WORKERS' COMPENSATION

STRATEGIES FOR LOWERING COSTS
AND
REDUCING WORKERS' SUFFERING

STRATEGIES FOR LOWERING COSTS

AND

REDUCING WORKERS' SUFFERING

Selected proceedings from conferences held in Lansing, Michigan
on April 22, 1987 and May 12, 1988

Sponsored by
School of Labor and Industrial Relations
Michigan State University
and
Bureau of Workers' Disability Compensation
Michigan Department of Labor

EDITED BY

EDWARD M. WELCH

LR

LRP PUBLICATIONS
FORT WASHINGTON, PENNSYLVANIA

LRP Publications
An Axon Group Company
Fort Washington, Pennsylvania 19034

Library of Congress Cataloging-in-Publication Data

Workers' compensation—strategies for lowering costs
    and reducing workers' suffering

    "Selected proceedings from conferences held in
Lansing, Michigan on April 22, 1987 and May 12, 1988,
sponsored by School of Labor and Industrial Relations,
Michigan State University and Bureau of Workers'
Disability Compensation, Michigan Department of Labor."
    Includes index.
    1. Workers' compensation--Congresses.   2. Industrial
hygiene--Congresses.   3. Health promotion--Congresses.
I. Welch, Edward M.   II. Michigan State University.
Bureau of Workers' Disability Compensation.
HD7103.6.W68   1989   368.4'1   89-2485
ISBN 0-934753-33-4

Manufactured in the United States of America

First Edition

Contents

PART FOUR: THOUGHTS FROM THE SCHOLARLY COMMUNITY

Contributors

Edward M. Welch

Director

Bureau of Workers' Disability Compensation

Michigan Department of Labor

Ed Welch has been Director of the Bureau of Workers' Disability Compensation since October 1985. Prior to that he practiced law, specializing in workers' compensation, social security disability and labor law. He has a J.D. degree in law from the University of Michigan.

His previous publications include *Workers' Compensation in Michigan: Law and Practice,* which was released in 1984 by the Institute of Continuing Legal Education in Ann Arbor. He has also written many journal articles. Mr. Welch has taught at the Graduate School of Labor and Industrial Relations at Michigan State University.

Leonard P. Sawisch, Ph.D.
Administrator, Office of Disability Management
Michigan Department of Management and Budget

Len Sawisch is currently Administrator of the state's Office of Disability Management in the Department of Management and Budget, on full-time loan from the Department of Education. The office is responsible for implementing a disability management system for state government — the third largest employer in Michigan — under the direction of a unique statewide Labor-Management Policy Council.

Dr. Sawisch received his Ph.D. in Developmental Psychology from Michigan State University in 1978. As a long-time advocate for handicapper issues, he currently serves as a special advisor to the National Council on the Handicapped, a member of the President's Committee on Employment of People with Disabilities' National Symposium on Employment of Americans with Disabilities, and the U.S. Olympic Committee representing disabled athletes. Sawisch has written for various rehabilitation and handicapper journals.

Don G. Tonti
Director
Michigan Disability Management Project

Don Tonti has been a human resources consultant as well as the Director of the Michigan Disability Management Project for several years. Prior to that he served as Corporate Director of Human Resources for Walbro Corporation — the period that served the basis for his contribution in this book. Other previous work experience includes being Industrial Relations Manager at General Tire and Rubber and Education/Training Administrator at United Air Lines.

He is currently an adjunct faculty member of Saginaw Valley State University, President of the Northwest Michigan Industrial Relations Association, and Vice-President of the Michigan Job Training Partnership Association.

Donald E. Galvin, Ph.D.
Senior Consultant
National Rehabilitation Hospital, and
Institute for Rehabilitation and Disability Management

Don Galvin is engaged in strategic planning, program development, policy studies and disability management research. He is currently co-principal investigator (with Willis Goldbeck of the Washington Business Group on Health) in a three-year research project dealing with corporate policies on disability management.

Previously, Dr. Galvin was a Professor in the School of Health, Counseling Psychology, and Human Performance, and in the College of Osteopathic Medicine at Michigan State University, where he was responsible for the graduate program in rehabilitation counselor education. He has also served as Associate Superintendent of Education and Director of the Michigan Rehabilitation Service. Among Dr. Galvin's pertinent publications is a chapter in the 1986 edition of the *Annual Review of Rehabilitation.*

Martha H. Miller
Workers' Compensation and Rehabilitation Administrator
Consumers Power Company

Martha Miller's current position in the Corporate Safety and Health Department at Consumers Power Company was preceded by positions that included responsibility for developing and implementing safety related programs and training. A graduate of Spring Arbor College, Ms. Miller has a B.A. degree in the management of human resources.

Ms. Miller is a member of the Michigan Coalition for a Safe Work Environment and the Community Advisory Board of the Department of Public Health's Pilot Worksite Health Promotion Project. For the last year and a half she has served on the Economic Alliance ad hoc group that has been working with Michigan's Department of Labor, Department of Management and Budget, and health care providers to develop and implement health care rules and a fee schedule which would assist in the containment of workers' compensation health care costs.

James C. Soule
Vice-President
Steelcase International

Jim Soule was appointed Vice-President of Steelcase International in July 1988 after having served as Vice-President of Human Resources at Steelcase, Inc. since 1984. Prior to that he was Regional Manager for Rohrer, Hibler, and Replogle, an international management consulting firm, where he had responsibility for the firm's offices in Detroit, Grand Rapids, Cleveland, and Toronto.

Dr. Soule has a Ph.D. in Psychology from Wayne State University and has taught at Wayne State, the University of Wisconsin-Milwaukee, and Wayne County Community College.

Kevin M. Meade
Industrial Relations Manager
DiversiTech General

Kevin Meade has been the Industrial Relations Manager of DiversiTech General (the Ionia, Michigan plant) since 1979. In 1984 when The General Tire and Rubber Company restructured, the Ionia plant became part of a wholly owned subsidiary of a newly formed holding company known as GenCorp. The subsidiary is DiversiTech General. The Ionia plant has approximately 600 hourly and 125 salaried employees. It is a major supplier of reinforced plastic body panels to the automotive industry.

Prior to becoming Industrial Relations Manager at DiversiTech General, Mr. Meade was an Assistant Personnel Director and Labor Relations Coordinator for the company. He received his B.S. in Psychology from Bowling Green State University.

Elizabeth P. Howe
Director
Michigan Department of Labor

Named to her current position for the state by Governor James J. Blanchard in February 1985, Elizabeth Howe assumed added responsibilities of the Michigan Employment Security Commission in August 1986. As a member of the Blanchard administration, Mrs. Howe serves on the Governor's Cabinet Council on Jobs and Economic Development and the Cabinet Council on Human Investment.

Prior to her state appointments, Mrs. Howe served as General Manager of the United-Nederlander Cable Television Company, was manager of Public Affairs for the Bendix Corporation, served as a private public relations consultant and as an editor or writer for *The Birmingham Eccentric* in Oakland County and for the J.L. Hudson Company. For several years Mrs. Howe also served on the Michigan State University Board of Trustees, but she resigned that position to avoid a conflict of interest prior to her newest state appointment.

John P. Miron
Chief Deputy Director
Bureau of Workers' Disability Compensation
Michigan Department of Labor

Jack Miron was first appointed Secretary of the Workmen's Compensation Department in 1957 by Governor Williams. Since that time he has been in the state workers' compensation hierarchy, from the private sector where he worked as a claims manager to having been appointed Acting Director of the Bureau five times — twice by Governor Romney, twice by Governor Milliken, and once by Governor Blanchard.

A graduate of Vanderbilt University, Mr. Miron is a past president of the International Association of Industrial Accident Boards and Commissions (IAIABC) and a current Regent of the IAIABC's Workers' Compensation College.

Patrick D. Cannon
Director
Commission on Handicapper Concerns
Michigan Department of Labor

Prior to moving to his current position Pat Cannon spent 13 years in government public service. During 1987 he developed and implemented a statewide outreach program for Michigan businesses, which included the Workers' Compensation Action Line he discusses in this book. Before beginning to work in public service, Mr. Cannon spent 13 years in broadcasting and 9 years in management.

Mr. Cannon is presently a member of the Meridian Township Cable Television Commission, the BoarsHead Theater Board of Trustees, the Capitol Area Transportation Authority's Local Assistance Program, and the Michigan School for the Blind's Citizens' Advisory Council, of which he is current Chair.

Ervin Vahratian
Deputy Director
Bureau of Workers' Disability Compensation
Michigan Department of Labor

Erv Vahratian has held the position of Deputy Director of the Bureau since 1968, except for the period of 1970-72 when he served as Director. A graduate of Wayne State University, Mr. Vahratian has a B.S. in business administration.

He is a past president of the Detroit Claims Manager's Association, the State Arbitration Council and the Michigan Claim Action Committee. He is also a member of the International Association of Industrial Accident Boards and Commissions.

H. Allan Hunt, Ph.D.
Manager of Research
The W.E. Upjohn Institute for Employment Research

Allan Hunt has been employed at the Upjohn Institute since 1978 and was appointed to his current position in 1982. His professional experience has involved him in the areas of workers' disability compensation, employment and training policy, and the employment impacts of technological change. He has consulted widely in Michigan on workers' compensation policy issues.

Dr. Hunt was educated at the University of Wisconsin, Lehigh University and the University of California at Berkeley, where he received his Ph.D. in Economics in 1974. He has taught at Lehigh University, California State University at Hayward, and the University of Connecticut. He is the author of *Workers' Compensation System in Michigan*, published by the Upjohn Institute in 1982.

Daniel R. Ilgen, Ph.D.
Professor of Organizational Behavior
Michigan State University

Dan Ilgen is currently the John A. Hannah Distinguished Professor of Organizational Behavior at Michigan State. He received his Ph.D. in industrial-organizational psychology at the University of Illinois at Champaign-Urbana.

He has served as President of the Society of Industrial and Organizational Pyschology and he currently serves as Associate Editor of the *Journal of Organizational Behavior and Human Decision Processes*. His research has addressed issues of leadership, work motivation, job satisfaction, absenteeism, and performance appraisal. He is a co-author of two books and either author or co-author of many professional articles.

Scott N. Swisher, M.D.
Professor of Medicine
Michigan State University

As Professor of Medicine Dr. Swisher has been instrumental in the development of a program in industrial health and occupational medicine, which provides the basis for the work presented here. This program is a collaborative effort involving the SAF in Stockholm, Sweden and both the Colleges of Human Medicine and of Business of Michigan State University. Dr. Swisher's M.D. comes from the University of Minnesota, where he studied electrical engineering before turning to medicine.

Dr. Swisher first came to Michigan State in 1967 to serve as the first clinical department chairman in the Department of Medicine of the newly founded College of Human Medicine, a position he held for ten years. Subsequently he served as Associate Dean for Research and Graduate Programs of the college, where he helped to develop a number of collaborative research programs between basic and clinical scientists.

Daniel H. Kruger, Ph.D.
Professor
School of Labor and Industrial Relations
Michigan State University

Dan Kruger is a Professor of Industrial Relations at Michigan State, where he has been on the faculty since 1957. He received the university's Distinguished Faculty Award in 1977. Earlier, after earning his Ph.D. at the University of Wisconsin, he went on to become Assistant Professor of Management and Director of Commerce Extension Services at the University of Alabama.

Dr. Kruger has consulted for the U.S. Department of Labor, has chaired the Michigan Manpower Commission, and has served as Special Advisor for Manpower Programs to Governor William G. Milliken. In addition, he was appointed by President Reagan as a member of the Federal Service Impasses Panel and has served as a factfinder and an arbitrator extensively in both the private and public sectors. He has written numerous professional articles in the area of human resources, collective bargaining, and grievance administration.

Acknowledgments

Of course, this book is primarily the product of the various contributors, and their efforts are deeply appreciated. There are, however, several other people whose help must be acknowledged. First and foremost I wish to thank Elaine Gruenfeld Goldberg, the General Manager of the Book Division of LRP Publications. Her patient assistance in reviewing the text and designing the form of this book has been very useful. She has been of invaluable aid in translating this series of speeches into a readable book.

In addition I want to acknowledge the overall efforts of Kenneth F. Kahn and LRP Publications. I am convinced that workers' compensation is an area in which there is a great need for more exchange of information. Ken's commitment to publishing in this area is an important contribution.

These conferences could never have taken place without the effort of Edward E. Anderson, Assistant Director of the Personnel Management Program Service with the School of Labor and Industrial Relations at Michigan State University. It was Ed who had the primary responsibility for organizing and presenting these conferences. I also appreciate the support we received from Theodore H. Curry, Associate Director of the Personnel Management Program, and Richard Block, Director of the School of Labor and Industrial Relations.

Finally, I want to acknowledge Kimberley Vaughn, Marvin Rhynard, and Karl Benghauser, members of my staff, who assisted in putting on these conferences and preparing this publication.

November 1988   Edward M. Welch
                                                   Lansing, Michigan

Introduction

It Is Possible!

Edward M. Welch

Are there really strategies that lower employer costs and reduce the suffering of workers, at the same time? The answer is clearly yes!

In Michigan, as in many states, we often hear complaints that a plant could move to a neighboring state and save money on its workers' compensation costs. It appears that there may be **intra**state differences in costs that are even greater, however, than the **inter**state differences. Michigan's Bureau of Workers' Disability Compensation has commissioned a study of these differences by H. Allan Hunt of the Upjohn Institute.

As Dr. Hunt suggests in Chapter Eleven of this book, it does appear that there are very significant differences between employers in the same industry within Michigan. His preliminary findings indicate that the number of claims filed at companies in the same industry within Michigan can vary as much as tenfold, and this striking difference appears to occur in virtually every one of twenty-nine different industries examined. These differences among Michigan employers appear to be related to such factors as safety practices, corporate climate and culture, and disability management.

It is interesting to compare this intrastate relationship to specific interstate differences. Consider Indiana and Michigan, for example. By some measures, Michigan's workers' compensation benefit costs are about twice those of Indiana employers. The difference between costs in Maine and

Indiana, on the other hand, is about sixfold: Maine's costs are about six times those of Indiana's.

Yet *within* Michigan the worst employers have ten times as many claims as the best employers.

What causes these differences? We do not know all the causes at this point, but we hope that research will show them to us. Some of the factors, we must concede, may be things over which employers have no control (such as geography or cultural differences). At the same time, though, it appears that there are significant factors that both employers and workers can control. Some companies are successfully using strategies that significantly reduce their costs, thereby giving them a competitive edge. The most encouraging news is that these cost-saving strategies seem to work to the benefit of both the employees and the businesses.

Safety is the first and most obvious factor. Those of us who are involved specifically in workers' compensation programs sometimes overlook this obvious solution. If no one were ever injured, there would not be any workers' compensation claims. The first and most important step in controlling workers' compensation costs and protecting employees is thus a comprehensive, effective safety program. Martha Miller of Consumers Power Company describes one such program in her article, "A Corporate Safety and Health Program: The First Line of Defense."

Of course, much more than safety is involved. I have come to believe that a great deal has to do with the relationship between the worker and the employer, both before and after an injury. People ask me why it is that someone who has been a loyal and devoted employee for many years decides to hire a lawyer and sue after suffering an injury. I like to answer this by using the example of the football player. Think of what happens when a football player is injured. The action stops. All attention is focused on the injured player. He is assured, "You'll be all right. We'll take care of you." He is applauded as he is taken off the field. Contrast this to what happens in most industrial settings. The foreman is told, "Joe thinks he hurt his back." What does the foreman say? Most likely something obscene.

Now of course this does not happen in all plants or with all supervisors. But where it does happen, it makes a big impression. In my years of practice representing injured workers I had many men and women tell me, "I only want what I have coming." Yet hundreds of others clearly wanted every penny they could get, were out for revenge, and would do anything to avoid returning to work at that plant. Two things appear to make the difference: one, the relationship between the company and the worker before the injury and, two, the way the worker is treated once the injury occurs.

To explore this difference, consider the return-to-work situation. The employee is released to return to work with restrictions. He or she is scared to death to go back. "They'll be out to get me. The least little thing that I do, they'll fire me." At the same time, the employer is afraid to take the worker back. "The least little thing that goes wrong, he'll holler 'comp'." Here we have a classic example of a situation in which both parties would profit by the employee's returning to work, but both are afraid to try. Both think they are at a disadvantage.

One company in western Michigan has a different approach. When it hears that an individual is about to be released to return to work, the worker gets a call from the supervisor. He or she is invited to have lunch in the plant a few days before the release. The worker sees his or her old workstation, talks with coworkers, sees what to expect, and is welcomed. Is it any wonder that this employer has a good record of getting people back on the job, that it keeps its costs down? The company is Steelcase and you can read more about its policies in the chapter by Jim Soule called "Commitment at Steelcase."

I have come to believe that employers should visit workers when they are home sick. During my years of practice, workers would often complain to me that although they put in many good years for a company, when they were lying on their back in the hospital for three months, no one came to see them. I used to reply that they could not expect that from employers, that their companies, in fact, did not care about them. Since becoming the Director of the Bureau, however, I have learned that there are companies that do care. They do send supervisors out to visit sick and injured workers. They do it, and they save money.

Some time ago I spoke to a group of people who employ "roughnecks" in the oil-drilling industry, and I suggested that it would be a good idea to send their supervisors to visit injured workers in their homes or hospitals. I expected these people to reject the idea out of hand; but their loss-control supervisor came up to me and said that he had been preaching the same thing for some time and that when an employer did this, it saved costs.

I have recently been reading *Love, Medicine, and Miracles* by Bernie S. Siegel, MD.[1] In this best-seller a surgeon talks about how hope, love, empathy, and a positive outlook can have an impact on cancer patients. He cites case after case in which these things were an important factor in the course of the disease. He describes situations in which men and women without hope were taken over by cancer and succumbed to the disease. He cites many other cases in which when the patient was given

---

[1]   New York: Harper and Row, 1986.

hope, the tumors actually shrunk, the cancer went into remission, and the patients triumphed over the disease.

If a positive, caring healer and supportive family and friends can have such an impact on cancer, what can they do for a bad back? There are, I think, very few cases in which the worker is outright lying about his or her injury, and the legal system deals with those few cases quite well. The claims-handling system also deals very well with the large number of cases in which the injury is clear and the symptoms proportionate to what we would expect. The difficult cases are those in which the worker clearly has some injury, but the pain is greater or lasts longer than would ordinarily be anticipated. It is these cases that are challenges for the employer, the claims adjustor, the families, and the workers themselves. We must examine every possible approach to healing these injured men and women.

What should one expect the company doctor to do? Should a doctor be tough and mean, or solicitous and sympathetic? Neither approach is necessarily correct, and there is probably a middle of the road that is most appropriate. To a large extent, many different personalities can do the job well. An employer should expect the doctor, however, to be interested and concerned about the workers and about its business. The doctor should be innovative and willing to try new ideas. A company that sends a large number of patients to the same doctor should expect that doctor to come to the plant once in a while to look at the jobs and to talk to the workers.

I often ask employers if they have ever been in the office of their company doctor. Have they observed how long the doctor makes the patients wait? Have they found the office clean? Would they go there themselves? Would they send their children there? Many times when I ask these questions, I am met with dead silence, but not always. I have been in offices of company doctors where I would go and where I have sent my children.

Often the key to disability management is an early return to work. Most of the people in the workers' compensation system are, by definition, workers. They are men and women who have supported themselves and their families by the strength of their back, the agility of their hands, or the exercise of other mental and physical abilities. When these people suffer an impairment, for the most part, they are strongly motivated at the outset to return to their productive jobs as quickly as possible. When they are forced by circumstances to sit home for long periods of time, their outlook changes. Fears and anxieties develop, their self-image is threatened, and they begin to receive a variety of secondary rewards for not working. As time goes by, it becomes harder and harder for them to return to productive employment. An early return to work should always be the goal, even though it cannot always be accomplished with ease.

4

Taking an injured worker back into a department can be a difficult proposition for the supervisor. Since the supervisor has standards to achieve and quotas to meet, he or she is often reluctant to take in a worker who is clearly not yet up to full capacity. A worker's fellow employees may often have the same concerns and questions.

Various strategies have helped companies deal with this situation. The first is something we should not overlook—the basic, altruistic tendency we all share. Sometimes we hesitate too much to appeal to the goodness that resides within each human being. Recognizing this, some companies simply point out to their supervisors and workers that they have an obligation to their brothers and sisters and that they must accept the ethical and moral responsibility of providing injured workers with opportunities and assistance. Of course, this strategy is only effective with workers if it is compatible with the general policies of the company.

A very different approach is sometimes needed. Companies may find that they can improve the situation of injured workers by changing their accounting system. If workers' compensation costs are spread throughout the entire company, there is no financial incentive to aid an injured worker. If the costs of an injury are charged back to an individual department, however, the supervisor there will be strongly motivated to get the injured individual back to the job as soon as possible.

Unions must also play a role in this process. Strict seniority rules can be a hindrance to finding lighter jobs for injured workers. One very large employer in Michigan for years had a policy that workers must be completely recovered and able to handle all their duties before returning to any job. At one point the company recognized the futility in this approach and changed its policy to encourage the return to work of partially restricted employees. It announced both the change and immediate implementation of the new policy without consulting its union. The union resisted, and the change in policy was a complete failure.

The seniority system is very important to organized labor in the United States. At the same time, it has been my experience that most unions are genuinely concerned about their fellow workers who have been injured on the job. When approached within the framework of collective bargaining, unions are nearly always willing to work with an employer to help deal with this situation. The important thing is that the union be part of the process.

Many employers are experimenting with various types of sheltered or transitional workshops. What it takes to make a transitional workshop function effectively (indeed what it takes to make any of these programs function effectively) is a commitment from top management and an

5

enthusiastic individual to run the program. To see what I mean, picture this. At one auto plant in Michigan, the supervisor of a transitional workshop goes to the other supervisors in the plant and points out to them that they are making a great deal of scrap. The supervisors reply, of course, that this is a natural part of their operations. The first supervisor emphasizes that there is lot of usable material mixed in with that scrap. The other supervisors respond that in order to salvage the good material, they would have to have someone "who did nothing but sit on his rear all day and sort through the scrap." This is exactly what the transitional workshop supervisor has, of course: a constantly changing group of three to ten people who, because of an injury, can temporarily "do nothing but sit on their rears all day." The scrap is hauled to his department, and his temporarily restricted workers sort out the good parts. He reports to the cost accountants the same as all the other department supervisors, and he demonstrates a profit for the company even without considering the savings in workers' compensation benefits.

Transitional workshops are effective for many reasons. Most obviously, they provide lighter work for employees who are temporarily incapable of meeting the full requirements of their regular jobs. In addition, they provide a temporarily more accepting atmosphere where workers can gradually readjust to the demands of the workplace. Sometimes these workshops work for surprising reasons. It has been said that some employees complained bitterly that they were unable to return to the full duties of their regular jobs until being told that they would be put into "sheltered workshops"; then they decided that they would like to try their regular work after all.

Not all problems can be solved after an injury. Much depends upon how a worker is treated when injured, but much also depends upon the overall attitude of the company and the relationship between the worker and employer before an injury occurs. One employer told me that his company has an index by which they measure the "quality of work life" in a plant. They have found, as one would expect, that there is a direct inverse relationship between the quality of work life and workers' compensation costs: When quality of work life is high, costs are low.

In his chapter, "An Attitude Problem," Kevin Meade describes the importance of a change of attitude in reducing workers' compensation costs at his company. Another changed approach, in a company that did not have a serious workers' compensation problem to begin with, is reported by Don Tonti. He tells the story of how a "Healthletics Program"(SM) drastically reduced his company's workers' compensation costs.

Many of these ideas are not really new. Insurance companies have been aware of them for a long time. They have often made concerted efforts to get their policyholders to adopt many of these practices.

Donald E. Galvin has been dealing with the concept of disability management for years. He provides a comprehensive review of it in "Disability Management: An Overview of a Cost-Effective Human Investment Strategy." Another scholarly analysis is presented by Daniel R. Ilgen and Scott N. Swisher in "An Integrated Approach to Health in the Workplace."

There is a growing number of private firms that offer to help employers deal with this aspect of workers' compensation. Often they are affiliated with hospitals or traditional rehabilitation firms. Of course, the overlap with rehabilitation is obvious.

Although these strategies must be implemented primarily by businesses and their employees, there are also things that government can do to help. In "View from the Top," Elizabeth P. Howe, Director of the Michigan Department of Labor, outlines the various steps that have been taken in Michigan to improve the workers' compensation situation. Leonard P. Sawisch demonstrates that dealing with the problem of disability is not as difficult as it may seem in his chapter, "Creating a Context for Disability Management." You are sure to enjoy this most entertaining piece.

One important objective is for injuries that do occur to be handled properly. Veteran workers' compensation specialist Ervin Vahratian gives advice on reaching this objective in "Thirty-One Ideas for Improved Claims Handling."

Litigation is often the most troublesome part of any workers' compensation system, but various forms of alternative dispute resolution have proved to be successful in reducing or avoiding litigation in Michigan. John P. Miron shows how these techniques have worked in "Problem Solving Through Informal Conferences and Formal Mediation."

When accidents are avoided, however, and disability reduced, it is essential to the business owner that this be translated into reduced insurance premiums. In "Could You Be Paying Less for Workers' Compensation Insurance?" Pat Cannon discusses the techniques available to Michigan businesses for taking advantage of our system of open competition to secure the lowest price for workers' compensation insurance.

One final topic, surely of interest to all of us, is treated by long-time labor relations analyst Daniel H. Kruger in "Ethical Issues Relating to Workers' Compensation."

The concept treated in this book—disability management—offers great potential toward improving the current workers' compensation scene. Yet many people who are responsible for personnel decisions of large employers are either not aware of this phenomenon or are, for some reason, prevented from implementing these kinds of policies. Certainly the public-at-large and even policymakers have little awareness of this approach, partly perhaps because there is little hard research that "proves" these methods to be cost effective and partly because there has been no attempt to educate them on these matters. This book and the two programs that led to it are an attempt to rectify this situation.

In recent times there have been certain trends in workers' compensation. Through the 1960s and 1970s the trend was to expand the availability of benefits and to raise their levels. During the 1980s the trend has been in the opposite direction: laws have been amended to restrict the availability of benefits and some states have even lowered the amount of benefits. To be successful in the future, we must adopt an entirely different approach. We must implement strategies that lower workers' compensation costs and reduce workers' suffering at the same time.

PART ONE

Disability Management

1

Creating a Context for Disability Management

Leonard P. Sawisch

The purpose of this chapter is to create a context for understanding the notion of disability and the various perspectives presented in this book. While such a context is useful, it can result in an idealistic, if not simplistic, treatment of the topic. However, since simplicity is my forte, I much prefer to leave the complex details to other authors while I focus the next few pages on creating a basic understanding of the four concepts that are critical to managing disability in the workplace:

- THE BIG BUGABOO (Reasonable Accommodations)

- I AIN'T NO DOCTOR (The Medical Model)

- A DIFFERENT APPROACH (The Systems Model)

- ONE SIZE FITS ALL (The Success Formula)

THE BIG BUGABOO

Let's begin with a simple working definition of Reasonable Accommodation:

> Any logical adaptation, addition or change to an individual's work environment, work responsibility, or work schedule to allow that individual to perform (or better perform) his or her essential job duties or functions.

I was having trouble putting this concept into perspective until I realized that circles were the answer. You see, I was in a book store the other day and I picked up a book on Zen. In the opening paragraph it said that Life, in fact Reality, was a circle: the end was really the beginning and the beginning was really the end. Greatly relieved I put down the book (confident that I had finished it) and realized that circles, or more accurately historical circles, were the answer.

Since the beginning of time, every single worker has been a restricted worker. As a state bureaucrat, I trace my roots to the first civil servants—a committee of cave dwellers sent out to kill a Mastadon (Mastadon, that's the bureaucratic term for hairy elephant). The committee returned shortly to report that they could not do the job without reasonable accommodations. They wanted adaptive equipment, which they referred to as "sticks and stones." And you probably know the story from here: the people carrying the stones felt they were working harder than the people carrying the sticks, and so we created Unions.

Now the purpose of unions was, and still is, to advocate for reasonable accommodations. First they wanted things like lights and ventilation in the factory. Then they wanted more personal accommodations, like a bathroom and maybe a chance to eat a little lunch some time during the day. Next they wanted changes in the tests. It seemed there were some folks, mostly from other caves, who could do the essential functions of the job but could not pass the entrance tests. Well, then later, when the left-handed people wanted their phones moved to the right side of their cubicles, we created Personnel Directors.

The purpose of personnel directors was, and still is, to find workers who can do the essential functions of the job without requesting too many accommodations. This has worked out pretty well. The personnel directors were finding workers who could do the job without too many accommodations, but they were mostly picking people who looked and acted just like they did. So we created Affirmative Action Officers.

Affirmative action was intended to bring a wider variety of people into the employment circle, in other words, to encourage more reasonable accommodations. And so it appeared that we had come full circle. But not quite. You see, only in the last decade have we come to make significant efforts to bring the "truly restricted" workers (those handicapped or disabled) into the circle.

Three points should be reflected on from this historical perspective. First, reasonable accommodation is a *worker* issue, *not* a *handicapper* issue. Second, since the beginning of time, every worker has been a restricted worker. So we are not talking about something new but rather about where we are on the continuum of differentness. And third, by extension, managers have historically provided accommodations.

The BIG BUGABOO occurs when we hear the word "disability," and for some reason forget our roots as managers and thus our wealth of experience with accommodations.

I AIN'T NO DOCTOR

Most of us have come to understand the concept of disability in a medical model. So it is important to explore this model. Let's take my dwarfism as an example: I am just over four feet tall. This is diagnosed as my "disability," which I acquired, by the way, in an early labor dispute. Actually it was my mother's labor, but the analogy is interesting.

Anyway, the medical model starts by assuming that there are Perfect Humans (or Perfect Workers, in this context). Those of us with "disabilities" somehow vary from that notion of perfection. And while none of us can actually define perfect workers, we know intuitively that they exist, based on the relative ease with which we can identify those workers who don't measure up—the workers with disabilities.

The disabilities are seen as interfering with the worker's ability to do stuff (Stuff I believe is the technical term). Keeping in mind that this is a result of the worker's assumed biological deficit, we go to our medical practitioners and ask them to do one of two things: fix the disability (fix the person, if you will) or certify that the worker can't do certain stuff. We call this "restrictions."

Now perhaps there was a time when this medical model was appropriate and when if we had workers with such "medical restrictions" we could justify dislocating them from the work force. But we suspect today that **13** this model has some problems. I mean you know you have a problem as an employer when you have to deal with the M.D.s, the P.T.s, the O.T.s, the C.R.C.s, and all those other medically related professionals. They work on the individuals and fix them up as best they can, then bring them back to you and say, "O.K. Here you go. Your turn. Now *you* manage the disability!"

Your logical response is to say, "Now wait a minute while I see if I understand this. You all went to college for what, maybe eight to ten years, to become experts on disability. Now you say you're done and it's *my* turn? How can you expect me to do this? I didn't go to college to learn how to work with these people! I AIN'T NO DOCTOR!"

But that doesn't matter. They leave the person with you anyway. Then when you look closer, you begin to realize that this "stuff" that your worker is not supposed to be able to do is influenced by a number of factors:

1. *The medical practitioner's experience with the "stuff" you do.* If your place of work happens to be a clinic, hospital, golf course, or real estate office, they probably know a lot about your stuff. Otherwise, it could be a little iffy.

2. *The payment source.* You are in business. The medical practitioner is in business. You know how long you will stay in business if you don't satisfy your customers. The medical practitioners know how long they will be in business if they don't satisfy their customers. This is not to suggest that medical practitioners are unethical, only to point out that they, like you, are human.

3. *Ego.* In our culture, medical practitioners have often been trained to believe "If I can't fix it, it must be pretty damn bad!"

4. *The practitioner's past experience with "disability" and disabled workers.* And it is not just the amount of experience, but the quality and context of the experience—which leads to the last factor.

5. *Prior litigation.* Not all of these factors will lead you to believe that you are dealing with a very objective situation. And you may begin to think, "There's got to be another way to look at this. There has got to be a different approach."

A DIFFERENT APPROACH

I too struggled with this idea of a different approach from a personal perspective, and I would like to share with you what I came to understand about the locus of this problem. The medical model suggests that the locus of the problem is in the person and we therefore spend our time and energy focusing on the person.

I feel somewhat like Luther in that the inspiration for me to understand this differently came from the privy. I am four feet, four inches tall (which actually is a lie for basketball, as I stand just under four foot three), and my spouse is about three foot nine. We were sitting around a number of years ago thinking "Hey, that's our bathroom in there; wouldn't it be nice if we could use it?" So for Lenette's birthday I built the floor of the bathroom up so that the "throne" was no more than nine inches from the floor. Now hold this thought for a minute.

When I find myself out in public and have to use the facilities, I search for the door with the shorter of the two names. I go in and balance myself precariously on the stool to do my business. When I'm done, I wash my hands, reach up for a towel, and watch the water roll down my arm. Then if I'm in the mood, I climb up on the wet sink to reach the mirror to comb my hair. Now society sees me in this situation and says "Isn't it a shame; isn't it too bad that God did that or that that happened!" They see me experiencing a problem and they blame it on me; they think that there is something wrong with *me*!

So you know what I do? I invite those people to my house to use my bathroom. It's great! The guys are there experiencing vertigo. People come out and their legs are all cramped up. And I'm the kind of guy who stands there and says, "My goodness, you're handicapped; you're disabled." Invariably the response is "Bull roar, it's the toilet!!"

The first time that happened it all came clear to me; I finally understood the double standard. When I, or people like me, experience a problem, we have been encouraged to blame ourselves, to feel that there is something wrong with our minds, with our bodies, or with the way we control our emotions. When other people have the same kinds of problems, however, they are encouraged to blame the environment. And so it dawned on me that I too could blame the toilet! I do not have a "disability," but I (or anyone) can experience disability in interaction with the environment.

If the reality of disability only exists in interaction with the environment, then you don't have to manage the disability! Now you can get your hands **15** on the situation. All you have to do is manage the interaction between your worker and the work environment. And after all, that's what managers do. From this perspective, you suddenly realize you can manage disability and you don't have to be a doctor!

I had an excellent example of this when I was first coming out of the closet as a Little Person. Actually it was a clothes hamper, but anyway I was at Michigan State University at the time and I saw a young woman outside the journalism building, obviously distraught. So I walked up to her and said, "Wow, you really seemed bummed out!" (That's the way we talked back then.) She said, "Yeah, I don't know what I'm gonna do. If I don't take this class in journalism, I won't graduate, and I can't get into the building!"

"Why? What's the problem?" I asked.

"Look at me," she responded. "I'm paralyzed from the waist down."

Being an engaging conversationalist, I initiated the following exchange:

> "Let me see if I understand this right. For a half a million bucks, we could hook you up to one of those computerized walking devices and then you could get into the building and take the class, right?"

> "Yeah."

> "But for five hundred dollars, we could build a ramp over those steps, and you could also take the class then, right?"

> "Yeah."

> "And so could anyone else using a wheelchair, right?"

> "Yeah."

> "And anyone using crutches, or a walker, or even someone pulling their kid in a wagon, right?"

> "Yeah."

> "Then why the hell are you blaming your body when the real problem seems to be right out here in the form of steps? It is certainly a lot easier (and cheaper) to manage the problem by seeing it as an interaction between you and your environment than it is by assuming the problem is somewhere in you!"

This is a **DIFFERENT APPROACH** to the concept of managing disability in the workplace, or anywhere else.

In the context of this different approach, we can now define disability management:

> Managing the interaction between "disability" and the work environment to maximize productivity and minimize cost.

If managing the interaction is the key, what are the sources of these challenging interactions? First are those employees who become handicappers. It is interesting to note that employers who offer long-term disability (LTD) insurance are more than likely paying out more for LTD than they are for workers' compensation, although the nature of the medical diagnoses are similar. Generally the pattern is 60 percent LTD to 40 percent workers' comp.

Next are those employees who are already handicappers. They may present a challenge when there is a change in jobs or a change-over in the line. If a handicapper's diagnosis or condition changes significantly, that may also present a challenge. Finally, job *applicants* who are handicappers may present a challenge. If you want to manage disability, you should make sure your system allows you to meet the challenges coming from all three of these sources.

In the disability management context, there are four major levels of management opportunities:

1. Health Promotion, or building your work force's tolerance to the effects of injury and illness.

2. Safety Promotion, or preventing injury and illness.

3. Maintenance, or addressing the needs of workers at risk of losing productivity.

4. Return To Work, or never really dislocating workers because of injury or illness.

Levels one and two are pro-active. Clearly anything you can do to avoid injury or illness is the most effective approach. At level three, as soon as you identify an interaction that is affecting either productivity or potential productivity, you can move to address it. Once a worker is dislocated, either in the physical or work culture sense, the price tag goes up because of the need to relocate. If you can get into a management set where you never really "lose" a worker, the long-term costs go down.

Interestingly, most of us find our attention drawn to level four when we think about disability in the work force. And while this is the bottom line, **17** it really needs to be seen in the full context of all four levels of management opportunity. This does not mean you have to have a full-blown system in place for all these levels, but whatever system you do have should be sensitive to each level.

With these four levels in mind, take a moment to review Figure 1. This is a partial list of professionals having something to do with disability management. Note two things. First, none of these professionals has a primary or secondary focus in all four levels. Second, all these professional perspectives claim to impact on the same bottom line! They all claim to help reduce lost time, increase productivity, avoid injury and illness, and reduce disability costs. The point is that they are looking at the same reality from different perspectives and thus none alone has all the right answers. If nothing else, knowing this can help you be a "smarter shopper" of services and perspectives.

ONE SIZE FITS ALL

Now we can discuss the ideal system or solution: what I like to refer to as ONE SIZE FITS ALL. All my friends in Little People of America, by the way, keep their eyes out for "one size fits all—or double your money back guarantee" offers, for obvious reasons. I suggest you assume a similar orientation toward this discussion.

A. Commitment

In most cases it is helpful to start with commitment to disability management at the top of your organization and have that commitment come from the top down. It is not always necessary to have that commitment from the top to begin with, however. My neighbor has this big Labrador Retriever, and on most issues this dog and I see eye to eye. The other day I walked behind the dog, grabbed his tail, and found that with some vigorous shaking I could actually wag the dog! Anyone anyplace in the system can have the same effect. It is not necessarily the best place to be standing; but if the commitment is there, the job can be done.

The nature of the commitment is also important. It should focus on protecting the equity the employer has built in each worker. This equity is reflected in terms of both financial and human costs. It's these latter costs that tug at your heart. When you understand the costs of not managing disability on the worker, the coworkers, the supervisor, the worker's family, and the community, it can help meld your sense of

Figure 1.

Professional Orientations

	Wellness	Prevention	Maintenance	Return To Work
Supervision		S	P	
Unions	S	P	P	S
Personnel			P	S
Benefits Mgt.			S	P
Ins. Claims		S		P
Work Comp. Law				P
Industrial Medicine	S		P	S
Rehab.			S	P
Occupational Therapy			S	P
Safety		P	S	
Industrial Hygiene	S	P		
Ergonomics		P	S	
Risk Manager		P		S

P = Primary

S = Secondary

commitment. Anyone in your organization who is not ultimately concerned about protecting the organization's equity in its workers perhaps ought not be there.

B. Incentives

Once you have a sense of commitment, you need to identify incentives for getting others involved in disability management. Four key groups of players for whom incentives should be considered include the workers, the managers, the unions, and the vendors or professional service providers. I don't mean to suggest that you send all these folks to Hawaii for three weeks, but rather that you be sensitive to what motivates their participation and that you eventually hold them accountable.

For example, the next time a vendor offers to sell you state-of-the-art power hand tools, say, "This product looks real good! Now share with me your ergonomic back-up information about these tools. Better yet, I'll give you a percentage of what we save over the next three years in carpal tunnel related expenses if you will agree to cover any increase in these costs after we begin using your tools." That provides both incentive and accountability!

C. Tools

After you have commitment and incentives in place, you need to provide some tools, primarily for your managers. Generally this means access to resources that facilitate managing the interaction between the worker and the work environment. Traditionally this includes ergonomics, wellness and safety programs, and medical and rehabilitation services. Again, all these resources need not be in-house; but where they are located and how they are to be accessed are critical. The key is not to expect your managers to be experts in all these areas. Rather, expect your managers to know when and how to seek experts.

D. Systems

To pull the tools and incentives together, a couple of relatively formal systems are needed. First is a well-defined accommodation policy and accompanying procedures. Keep in mind that the underlying concept of this whole disability management area is accommodation. Also keep in mind that having and following your policy may prove to be the most important "cover your butt" resource you have if and when a "disability dispute" results in litigation.

Second is a system for identifying and tracking your people and the organization's costs relative to those people. If you are not tracking the amount and costs of lost time, for example, how would you ever know if things got better or worse? Without such a system it is also hard to know if your vendors are giving you a deal, or the business. And, of course, your managers will respect whatever the organization inspects.

Just a closing thought on systems: customer service. Everyone working directly or in an adjunct role to support disability management should realize that customer service is their business and their customers are the disabled workers and their supervisors or managers. That's the level where disability is first to be noticed and where the interaction effects will be the strongest.

E. Faith Healers

We are talking about a change in the way we look at things. We are talking about a change in attitude. When you look closely at successful systems or programs, invariably you find one person or a small group of people who were the faith healers in that organization—who appreciated the depth of change needed and who were willing to weather the storms such changes brought. Having the right people running your programs or supporting your programs is probably more important than the programs themselves.

SUMMARY

The purpose of this paper was to provide a context for understanding disability management. For those readers who always read the summary first, here are the four key concepts:

- Accommodation is not a handicapper or disabled person issue; it is a worker issue (and all workers are restricted workers).

- Disability is only relevant in interaction with the environment, and managing worker-work environment interactions is a management forte.

- Disability management, when all is said and done, is really just people management, and everyone in an organization is responsible for protecting the organization's equity in its people.

- Ultimately, disability management success is a matter of attitude, and your business's physical and cultural environment both supports and reflects the attitude you have.

of people who were the faith healers in that organization—who appreciated the depth of change needed and who were willing to weather the storms such changes brought. Having the right people running your programs or supporting your programs is probably more important than the programs themselves.

SUMMARY

The purpose of this paper was to provide a context for understanding disability management. For those readers who always read the summary first, here are the four key concepts:

- Accommodation is not a handicapper or disabled person issue; it is a worker issue (and all workers are restricted workers).

- Disability is only relevant in interaction with the environment, and managing worker-work environment interactions is a management forte.

- Disability management, when all is said and done, is really just people management, and everyone in an organization is responsible for protecting the organization's equity in its people.

- Ultimately, disability management success is a matter of attitude, and your business's physical and cultural environment both supports and reflects the attitude you have.

2

Healthletics Program ^{SM} [1]

Don G. Tonti

I would like to introduce you to a new concept—something we implemented at Walbro Corporation and refined through our work at other industries both inside and outside the State of Michigan—called Healthletics ⓢ. Our hope is that you can take this concept into your specific environment to see what it can do for your company and your people.

To begin to understand this concept, consider a football stadium. It is an environment in which we don't even use regular grass these days, where we force individuals to play on a padded rug before thousands of people (millions, considering television) who applaud their moves.

Now consider how we take care of these individuals, and you will get an introduction to our concept. These players, who are probably about 19 to 21 years old, have been taken care of ever since they grew to be clearly bigger than most other people. We've fed them and clothed them; we've said that they don't have to be smart, all they have to do is be big, and we'll take care of them, physically. And we've hired people to do that 24 hours a day, every day of their lives.

How have we done it? We've done it with a concept pictured in Figure 1, which shows a coach, a doctor, and the athlete, all corresponding through

---

[1]   Healthletics Program ⓒ is a registered servicemark of Athletic Training Services, Inc.

Figure 1.

Athletic Sports Medicine
Communication Triangle

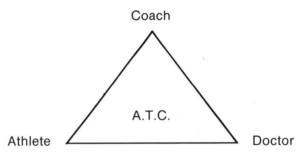

A.T.C. = Certified Athletic Trainer

a certified athletic trainer (ATC). This trainer works hard to coordinate and provide the care of this individual who plays on the field.

For the sake of later comparison, let's consider how much work a typical player does. We timed Jim McMahon (the Chicago Bears quarterback) in the championship game a couple of years ago and he played a total of about 8 1/2 minutes. So he expended 8 1/2 minutes of his time in a game, one day a week. He may play 14 to 16 weeks out of the year, and his career might last 5 to 10 years.

Think about that a minute and compare a defensive lineman, or one of your forwards on a basketball team, or your number one pitcher on the softball field to a typical worker at Walbro, or at your company. The athlete plays one to two days a week in certain seasons. The worker works five or six days a week, all year (50 weeks), 8 or sometimes 10 hours each day. For how many years? Maybe 30.

Let's see what companies normally do to assure that their workers' bodies enable them to do their jobs. Consider one of our employees at Walbro. We have a woman who has worked for us for over 30 years. In her job she performs about 6,000 to 8,000 repetitions a day. How have we treated her? Well, after she woke up at whatever time in the morning, 5:00 or 6:00, and took care of her husband, had his kids, and fed him and the kids and got them off to work and school, then we allowed her the privilege of coming to work at 7:00 or 8:00 in the morning. We allowed her to spend a nice leisurely day with a wonderful foreman who took care of her and a company that really cared for her, as yours do, I am sure. And when she got home she made dinner and listened to her husband complain about his bad day at the office and tried to solve the kids' problems and help them with their studies. And what else did we do for her? Good question!

We in industry need to consider what happens to workers after 6,000 repetitions a day, 5 days a week, 50 weeks a year, for 30 years. Or to those who work with an automatic drill, for example, after that drill forcefully comes to a stop. Or to workers in heavy industry who are using their backs so many times a day, picking things up, or typists or stenos who are sitting in an awkward position at their desks for 8 hours a day with typewriters or with CRTs. We need to have somebody in industry who understands those parameters. That's where our concept comes in.

Now, take the picture in Figure 1 and replace the coach with management and the athlete with your employee (see Figure 2). What the Healthletics Program℠does for Walbro is to call the employees "industrial athletes" and to treat them and their entire environment as if they are the individuals we saw on the football field, the basketball court, or the baseball diamond. At Walbro we took the concept of "sports medicine" and we provided our employees the same type of atmosphere that the athletes had.

Let's explore what I mean. After a game, the news media are allowed to go right into the locker rooms to talk to any of the players or any of the managers. There is only one place they cannot go, and that is into the trainer's room—because that area is sacrosanct, that is where the athlete goes so that he or she can get away from the rigors of what is required by the job.

We wanted to create a similar oasis, a place where our individuals could go to get away from a problem and to seek help from a caring, concerned expert. We felt that what we wanted could come from certified athletic trainers (ATC) because they could maintain daily contact with any or all of our employees and could act as resource people to whom our employees could go with their injuries, their illnesses, and their problems. What we found was that the trainers were able to apply therapy to help employees recover from strains, avoid sprains, and improve their health through supervised exercise or fitness programs. We found they could help our employees modify their lifestyles.

For an athlete with a sprain or strain, the whole idea of using a trainer is to have that No. 40 get back into the game as soon possible. What we have done under this concept at Walbro is use this trainer to take an injured employee, relieve the pain, and get him or her back on the job as quickly as possible.

Take our corporate loan officer, for example. She tripped down a few stairs in her high-heeled shoes and suffered a severe ankle sprain. In an ordinary working situation, she would have gone to a physician to complain about the sprain—whether it was an ankle or a knee or a wrist—and the physician would have said, "Well, how badly does it hurt? Why don't you stay home, keep ice on it, keep it elevated and still for two weeks, and then come back and see us? We'll see how you feel at that point."

Figure 2.

Industrial Sports Medicine
Communication Triangle

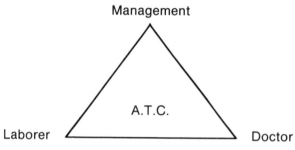

A.T.C. = Certified Athletic Trainer

Note the difference with our Healthletics ^{SM} approach. The employee may go to a physician—or to the trainer, first, and then to a physician if necessary. Once examined, however, the physician can refer the employee back to the facility with his diagnosis to have the company trainer work with him or her. An injured employee like the loan officer described above, for example, can come in every day or several times a day, for whatever treatment is necessary. The key is that that employee stays at the workplace. So you are not losing an employee for a day, or many days.

Of course, along with the trainer you must set up a training room, as we did, with the appropriate equipment for treatment. At Walbro we put in a whirlpool, ultrasound equipment, a Transcutaneous Electrical Nerve Stimulation (TENS) unit, and a hydroculator for warm, moist heat—plus equipment that functioned either for therapy or for fitness.

What we found was that the whole atmosphere at Walbro was so positive that we stopped distinguishing between occupational and non-occupational injuries or needs, and we opened up our facilities fully for all needs for all our employees *and* their dependent family members. And we experienced no abuse whatsoever. Employees with non-occupational needs come in on their lunch hour, before work, or after work.

Why Apply This Concept?

Let's take one individual to illustrate the savings potential. The example I use was not an employee: he was the spouse of an employee who was covered by our group medical program. A skilled tradesman, he is about 6 foot 5 inches tall. He had been diagnosed as having Guillain Barr'e Syndrome, which is basically a shutdown of the motor system. If this disease starts at the neck and goes down, it completely paralyzes you. If it goes up, it kills you. He was lucky: his went down. He was declared totally and permanently disabled. He was told that he would never have more than 75 percent use of his extremities again.

For the first 11 months of outside treatments for this patient, we spent upwards of $285 per treatment for therapy. We had already spent $195,000 on the disease and the therapy when the patient's wife asked if he could come in and go through the therapy in our on-site training room. After about 12 to 13 months of therapy in our facility, he was recovered to within 98 percent! He was coming in four days a week, having all of this done in-house, and without our spending one more penny on him, he became completely rehabilitated. He and his wife, in fact, have moved to Florida, and he is back to working in construction again. That individual alone saved us all the money it took to put our program in place.

We used to have an average of approximately two to three carpal tunnel surgeries a year with our employees. In October 1985 we put in a machine that we use for carpal tunnel problems; we initiated a preventative fitness program; and we began to apply ergonomics to those jobs that had previously caused us problems. Since the start of this program, we have not had one carpal tunnel surgery.

Why use sports medicine in industry? Basically, records from the Michigan Occupational Safety and Health Act (MIOSHA) show that just over 45 percent of all workplace injuries are sprains and strains (see Figure 3). If you include contusions, you actually hit over 50 percent. A certified athletic trainer can take care of all sprains, strains, and contusions—injuries that are reported as compensable cases to MIOSHA.

What about the distribution of our compensable cases? Approximately 85 percent occur in the extremities of the body (see Figure 4). Of the compensable cases reported, only 48 percent were actual on-the-job injuries. About 52 percent were what would be considered "program related." This latter group included accidents that occurred in the parking lot or were an aggravation of a prior injury, for example, and those that had some effect on activity outside of work. Almost 70 percent of our total compensable cases were in the group of employees we would expect to be the healthiest, the 20-44 age group.

Figure 3.

Percent Distribution of Compensable Cases by Nature of Injury or Illness

Sprain/Strain	45.3%
Fracture	12.5%
Cuts/Lacerations	10.5%
Contusions	8.8%
Occup. Disease	7.3%
Burn-heat	2.1%
Amputations	1.2%
Abrasions	1.1%
Burn-Chemical	.4%
All others	10.8%

After we were about six months into our program, over 43 percent of our employees were involved in some type of fitness program with our company. (I think that has expanded now to almost 50 percent.) That happened without any type of incentives: without paying them to stop smoking, and without paying them to go to aerobics classes. That is what those employees are doing on their own initiatives.

Figure 4.

Percent Distribution of Compensable Cases by Part of Body Affected

Back	24.5%
Fingers	11.0%
Knee	6.2%
Hand	5.8%
Abdomen	4.9%
Arm	5.1%
Wrist	4.6%
Ankle	4.4%
Foot	3.7%

Source: MIOSHA Information Section, Michigan Department of Labor

Approximately 31 percent of all injuries are caused by overexertion or fatigue. Also, according to MIOSHA's injury and illness reports, the highest number of complaints traditionally occur on Monday. Once we at Walbro stopped separating our occupational and non-occupational cases and had our trainer in place, we experienced an interesting change. The first Monday of April in 1986, which it so happens followed the first beautiful weekend of the spring, our trainer saw nine employees who came in before work. Every one of them had gotten hurt over the weekend, either playing softball or some other game or starting to jog again. It is quite likely that prior to this change many of these people would just have waited and come in a half-hour later, saying they had slipped on the stairs or injured their back lifting something, and reporting it as an occupational injury. Why would they do that? Because economically we make it more feasible for them to deal with it that way. When we change that, however, they start reporting it exactly as it was.

SAVINGS EXPERIENCED

Let's see what we were able to do at Walbro. Between 1985 and 1987, while the average employment went up over 16 percent, total workdays lost went up by only 6 percent (See Figure 5). Days lost per employee went down 13 percent!

Figure 5.

Walbro Corporation
Trends in Injuries, Days Lost, and Costs
Between 1985 and 1987

Average Number of Employees	up	16.7%
Workers' Compensation Days Lost		
Total days lost	up	6.02%
Days lost per employee	down	13.6%
Injury cases	up	38.0%
Workers' Compensation Costs		
Wages	down	73.5%
Medical payments	down	39.3%
Total Cost	down	61.3%
Cost per employee	down	64.4%

The most significant thing, however, was what happened to our workers' compensation costs. The amount we were paying out in wages for workers' compensation time off in 1985 went down 73 percent and medical payments went down 39 percent by 1987. The total cost of our entire program, including reserves, went down 61 percent. When we look at it per employee, based on the increase in employees, the cost of our total program went down 64 percent.

There is another way to look at this concept. For a moment, you should look at your employees the same way you look at your machinery. You are often accused of treating your employees just like machines anyway; so for a moment, do so. There is an optimum life performance you would like to get out of your machinery, let's say of 100,000 hours. Without maintenance that life will drop, and you will get only a percentage of those workhours from that machine, possibly 85,000 hours.

The same is true with your employees. With the kind of Healthletics℠ atmosphere we have created, you can get 80 hours a week of top performance out of your employees. They are there every day with very little time off. Without a maintenance program, without watching their slight injuries and illnesses, without having someone there to take care of them, that performance drops down, according to our statistics, to 65 hours.

A company formed by former athletic trainers at Central Michigan University, called Athletic Training Services (Mt. Pleasant, Michigan), refers to an injury index ratio. Let's consider this injury ratio index for a minute. To derive the index you must figure out how many widgets or whatever your employees would be producing during their lost time. How? Well, your team one employee produces at a certain rate. That employee has a "mean time to failure," which means that after producing that rate of widgets for a certain period of time, that employee's body will start to reject some aspect of the performance it is required to do: either the repetition or carrying heavy weights or something. The result will be time lost or poor performance due to disability. What you are doing then by using the Healthletics℠ program is saving time by extending your employees' mean time to failure.

Recently we have begun studying this concept in more detail. This analysis focuses on the team aspect of Healthletics℠, and we have been exploring it in about 70 companies that have used some sort of injury intervention program. Most companies, like most sports, function as teams. Each company has its star line-up, its first team, which is made up of its most productive employees (usually about 20 percent). They produce at a rate of, say, 1,000 units per hour. But not everything they produce is perfect, and so we have what is called a "rejection rate" for the first team. Let's say that for Company X (the average in our study) that rejection rate is 2.73 units per hour. For whatever they produce, whether it is typing, manufacturing computers, or sweeping the floors, their rejection rate is 2.73 units per hour.

When we compare the first teams in most companies with their second teams, however, we find large differences, not so much in the rate at which they produce as with the rate of widgets they must reject: instead of about a 2.7 rejection rate, we get a 21.0 rejection rate! Now there is nothing that says that you can make these second team players into first team players. You can't do that, just as the Detroit Pistons can't take some of their players from the bench and turn them into Isaiah Thomases. But what you can do through a Healthletics Program ^(SM), it turns out, is reduce that rejection rate. Our experience has shown that you can reduce that rejection rate from 21.0 to 16.7 percent, for a 30 percent improvement.

Our study results show that by using Healthletics ^(SM) to treat employees for all of their minor sprains and strains and to work with them on maintenance programs for their physical abilities, the most significant result is a large drop in the rejection rate. The program cannot make second team employees work at first team rates. They still must work at their own rate, which is what they are capable of doing. But apparently through feeling better about themselves and being better physically, employees reduce their scrap errors and thus become more efficient.

PRIMARY ADVANTAGE

What is the primary advantage then to a corporate on-site Heathletics Program ^(SM)? Reducing workers' compensation time lost by using early intervention techniques.

We were puzzled by what happened when we first put our program in at Walbro: our sprains and strains increased to 70 to 80 percent of all injuries reported during the first two years. The first year I think it was 70 or 75 percent, and the second year it was 80 percent. What was happening? Our employees were coming in with their minor sprains and strains so that we were able to treat them when they were still minor and to correct them on site at the facility before they became major problems that required taking time off. Minor injuries generally have no lost time and a short-term recovery rate (daily access to an on-site facility helps).

In addition to corrective therapy we have been able to put in exercise programs at the employees' request, programs they use on their own time. There was one small employer I was working with that instituted an exercise program and about a month later I asked their manager what their participation rate was. He said it was 100 percent and I said, "My gosh, that is just fantastic!" Since they were not a very well-managed company, I was really impressed and I thought, See what a little bit of encouragement will do.

I said, "Well, that is not every day because there are other things they have to do."

"Oh, yeah," he says, "that is every day. The boss said if he is going to pay for something, every single employee must use it!"

So you see what we sometimes do as management: we overreact. The same thing I think has happened in our workers' compensation situation throughout industry. We overreact to that minority of employees who cause us the biggest set of problems rather than worrying about the majority of employees, who don't.

The majority of all our employees are looking for reasonable ways to resolve their problems, whatever they may be. They, like you and me, want to work but don't want to hurt while working. They would like to feel good. They would like to get quick relief if something hurts. They would like not to waste their time. They would like to be secure about their incomes, if something happens to threaten their jobs. A program like a Healthletics Program(SM) enables them to do all these things in a way that assists their employers in maintaining a well-functioning workforce and keeping costs to a minimum.

QUESTIONS AND ANSWERS

You mentioned a reduction of carpal tunnel surgery in 1985. What was the machine you used for that?

Originally we did not have any special equipment. At first we were doing what the rest of the industry was doing: putting on warm compresses. Since our athletic trainers were trained in ergonomics, they would go out to the work site to observe the operation that was creating the carpal tunnel problem and observe what the employees were doing and how they were doing it. Then the trainers would use their expertise to redesign the position or what the individuals were doing so that they would use the entire arm, for example, rather than just the wrist.

Later we were able to find a piece of equipment that works through the nervous system. I am just a layman, not a doctor, but let me try to explain how it works. A carpal tunnel problem arises from inflammation causing a closure within the tunnel; it can occur anywhere up through the shoulder although it is most common in the wrist. Well, the equipment (Electro Accuscope Myopulse) we have now takes a reading of where and what percentage of the closure in the nerve conduction is and sends small impulses through that help to reduce the inflammation within the nerve tunnel.

In the meantime, through a fitness program we build up the other muscles in the body. Just like a football player who does not throw with just his arm and has to put his whole body into a block, it is appropriate for employees to put every part of their bodies into the action they are doing. So far with this routine, we have been lucky enough to stay away from any further carpal tunnel surgeries.

Did it reduce the incidence of carpal tunnel in the workplace?

We are not sure. Our program was bottom-line oriented, and we are not so complex as to know how many incidents were actually reported. We just know what the bottom line is and that the people were happier with it. Our biggest savings came about, we feel, because we took the things that our trainer knew right to the floor, not only to the individual, but also to the supervisor. We let the supervisor know what our trainer knows: Are the stations too high or too low? Does the individual have to do something that is awkward as opposed to something more natural.

So now we have supervisors who are semi-expert in that area. They are looking for those types of things, for example. They will not allow their employees to work with their wrist hanging on a sharp edge. A lot of it is common sense and that is what we reduced it to.

Quite frankly, what we feel we have developed is more concern about our situation, and this carries through into my current work with the state government. Originally people thought that with state employees, nobody cared who was off or how much it was costing. Well, I am finding out that they do care. The problem is that nobody in the system had put it all together and asked what could be done about it. Basically all we have done in this disability management project is to gather the concerned departments that have most of the problems and put the systems together to see how we as a group can best handle it. We brought it in-house, relying—rather than on the medical profession that cares and wants to do something but is trained to give medicine and recommend rest—on the profession that understands the parameters of the physical being through correct usage.

When the employees use the equipment, is a trainer available?

Yes. We have taken some simple precautions. No one is allowed in the training room without a trainer. No one is treated without a physician's statement, and no one starts a fitness program without signing a waiver that there is nothing wrong with them. We started out by requiring that every individual interested in doing a fitness program go to their doctor and have a physical; but we got a lot of complaints about the cost of the physical, and so we just have them sign a waiver. Basically many of these activities that I credit to the certified athletic trainer originally came to us from a physician's diagnosis and prescription authorizing some type of therapy.

Do you have any idea what the costs are of implementing and maintaining such a program?

Yes. Walbro had only about 700 employees, 300 at one location, 250 about 15 miles away, and another 100 or so 20 miles away. We figured when we first talked to the people from Athletic Training Services that because we had a good safety record and had so few workers' compensation injuries we might need a trainer part-time. We were either going to hire a part-time trainer or hire someone full-time and send him out to the local high schools when he was not busy.

Well, let me tell you this. Right now we have facilities at all three of our locations and we have three full-time trainers and two interns. With all that, all the salaries plus incidentals plus whatever they budgeted for their equipment—the entire thing was paid for in the first 10 months of our program.

What is the cost per employee?

When we first got into this, we were interested in getting in on the fitness fad, like a lot of you are, and then we thought, well, maybe we can save a couple of pennies by working on our own workers' compensation. So we looked at our own costs. They were $112 per employee per month. In Michigan in 1985 the average was $226 per employee per month; so we were 100 percent better than the rest of the state to begin with. Some might wonder why we did anything.

The first year we had our system in operation, our costs went down to $58 per employee per month. In 1987 the cost reached $36. Remember, there is not one individual who must be treated by the trainer. No one is forced to go in there. For any workers' compensation problem, the employee can still go to the physician we select and if that physician or the employee wants to use different therapy, that is fine. We do not insist that the employee use this system.

We have been so successful with it, however, that we are now using it for all of our group medical. So individuals on our medical plan can come here and be treated for minor sprains and strains, 100 percent paid for. It's already there. Or they can go to their physician and let someone else treat them, and in some cases it will be 100 percent covered and in others, 80 percent. No one is forced to use our services.

Can an individual with a minor sprain or strain get a prescription from the doctor?

A majority of the time individuals either go to the doctor first and get a prescription for the treatment or, if they come to the trainer first, the trainer calls the physician (their physician or, if they do not have one, one he or she selects) to give an analysis of what he has found and to get guidance. The physician will either give the trainer written authority or correspond with the trainer or the individual will be sent to the physician to be looked at.

Another question that often comes up is what our concern was at Walbro regarding malpractice liability or that type of thing. We were not afraid. We attacked the program as if we kept it in-house: we kept it close, we knew what we were doing, and we did not force anyone to participate. We have all the records right there of everything we are doing and anyone who wishes to question it can. So if there is any type of lawsuit or any type of malpractice that is filed against us, we feel we have all the records there to show exactly what we have done. We have never had any, but that is not to say that we never will. We just feel we are better covered by doing it right there and being up front with everything we are doing.

Were you self-insured?

Yes, we were and are self-insured.

What would you anticipate?

It is too soon to declare, but it is safe to assume that your insurance premiums will decrease. Walbro's Group Medical administrative rates were reduced dramatically in the third year of the program. The best thing we experienced, however, was in the immediate improvement in time lost.

This is a question from a physician's perspective. Does the person who is injured need to be reviewed by the physician before going to the athletic trainer?

Generally, yes, that is the case, unless the employee expresses only a mild   **35** discomfort. If there is any doubt, the trainer refers the employee to a physician.

How were your cost savings realized in terms of medical care, if the individual still has to go to the physician? Is it just that instead of sending the patient to physical therapy, you are now sending him or her to the trainer?

That is correct, but it is no different from workers' compensation.

So the cost saving is realized because the trainer has already been paid for?

Well, that is part of it. The other part is that when the therapy is no longer necessary, these people are either not taking time off or are coming back to work sooner, and they are not having the same frequency of visits to the physician that they previously had. The physician wants someone to look at the injury to see what is happening (Is the swelling going down? for example), but rather than requiring the patient to return to his or her office to be checked during this interim period, the physician relies on the trainer to do the checking until the physician finally releases the patient.

I think another thing that is important to point out in a program like yours is that the trainers can be very helpful to the physicians, many times guiding them. Often in normal physician-patient interactions, the physicians have no idea when they are dealing with work-related problems or what the progress of those problems is.

At Walbro we did not have an in-house physician; we had about 70 physicians in the area we were dealing with. Before we put the program in, we invited them all in for a briefing to explain what we intended to do. Only half a dozen or so attended, and we had questions from each of them. Once we got started, for each situation we would send out a letter saying, You have a patient who is our employee, we have these facilities, and we would like to treat this patient.

I can tell you that there was not one of them who took it at point-blank value and responded, "That's great; treat them." Every one of them investigated our program until he or she became comfortable with what we were doing. By now, both they and their patients feel comfortable with what we are doing.

We have worked with larger companies that have a physician on staff. They are realizing a good savings with the physician on staff referring to the trainer.

Do you have employees who have not felt comfortable or have been displeased with it?

We have nothing that even tracks that. What happens though is that as the trainer is working with an employee, the trainer will refer back to the employee's physician or to another one. There are no rules that say the employee cannot go to a physician at any time. So, an employee can do both if he or she wants to.

3

Disability Management: An Overview of a Cost-Effective Human Investment Strategy

---

Donald E. Galvin

INTRODUCTION

Disability management and rehabilitation initiatives are driven by, and operate within, a complex system including demographic trends and the economic forces of the labor market and the health care industry. In a very real sense, such trends and forces set the "ecological" stage in terms of enhancing opportunities and incentives for disability management, rehabilitation and return to work, or conversely creating overwhelming obstacles and powerful deterrence to such efforts.

Joseph Califano reports that American employers spend approximately $91 billion each year to provide health insurance for more than 130 million workers and family members, up from $15.5 billion little more than a decade ago.[1] Moreover, these costs are likely to increase sharply as the American work force grows older. Thus the business community, the payor of more than half of the nation's total health care bill, understandably has a great stake in controlling the cost of health care and rehabilitation. Further, as the principal payor for health care and rehabilitation services, employers have a responsibility to assure that they are purchasing high quality services on behalf of their employees.

This is a report on disability management as a cost-effective human investment strategy for business and industry. It will begin with a review of the forces that are driving this new dimension of workers' compensation rehabilitation. Then it will identify and discuss the critical elements of the disability management strategy and highlight the significant trends and innovations in the field. At the end it will discuss a few of the more troublesome problems and conflicts in the area.

Forces Driving the Interest in Change

The primary forces that are currently driving corporate interest in disability management are significant cost factors. Among them one would note the following:

- The escalating costs of employer-sponsored health, disability, and compensation schemes.

- The demographic bombshell known as "The Graying of America," which will have a profound impact on the country, most particularly on employers.

- The changing pattern of disability incidence and prevalence.

- Expensive medical technologies that save and sustain lives.

Costs Associated with Benefit Schemes

Robert Reich, a Harvard policy analyst, notes in his book *The Next American Frontier* that U.S. employers provide social and health services equal to approximately 20 percent of all publicly sponsored human services.[2] They not only underwrite medical care and wage replacement; some also provide child care services, exercise and health promotion programs, retiree services, nutritious subsidized food, and employee assistance programs for those with alcohol, drug, and other personal

---

[1]   Joseph A. Califano, Jr., *America's Health Care Revolution: Who Lives? Who dies? Who Pays?* (New York: Random House, 1986).
[2]   New York: Penguin Books, 1983.

problems. In fact, employers are now on the cutting edge of such major public policy questions and challenges as neonatal care, elder care, organ transplants, drug testing, and AIDS management. In a very real sense our de facto national health and social insurance policy has as its foundation our attachment to the labor market.

By offering health benefits and adopting positive human resource policies, companies are attempting to maintain worker health and productivity. In recent years many major firms' health care benefits have expanded to include major medical and hospitalization coverage, prescription drugs, dental care, vision care, drug abuse and alcoholism treatment, home health services, and hospice care. In addition, many companies have extended coverage to employee dependents, and most large employers now assume the cost of health insurance to supplement Medicare coverage for their retirees .

Yet, due to mounting foreign competition, American industry can no longer simply pass the cost of such benefits along to the consumer. In fact, according to economist Lester C. Thurow, "American industry is losing its markets at current prices and must reduce costs and prices if it is not to be run out of business. . . . Managing health care costs will continue to be a central business objective for at least the next five years."[3]

Nowhere in the American economy is this observation more germane than in Michigan, with its prominent role in the highly competitive automobile industry. Nearly one out of every three automobiles currently purchased in the United States is a foreign import. As a result, Michigan's dominant industry has a relatively new, but profound, interest in health care and compensation cost containment, for such benefits have become a major cost of doing business in the state.

In Michigan, employer spending on health benefits for active employees increased from $2.2 billion in 1977 to $5.2 billion in 1986. Health benefit costs have in fact been rising faster than any other benefit expenditure paid by employers.[4] Lee Iacocca, on becoming chairman of Chrysler Corporation, discovered that it was Blue Cross/Blue Shield of Michigan— rather than U.S. Steel or Goodyear Tire and Rubber—that was the company's leading supplier. In 1984 Chrysler had to sell 70,000 vehicles just to pay its health care bill!

Nationally, workers' compensation costs—now at nearly $35 billion annually—have more than tripled for many employers over the past five

---

[3]   Lester C. Thurow, "Medicine Versus Economics," *New England Journal of Medicine*, 313 (10), 611-13.
[4]   Donald E. Galvin, "Labor Market Economics: Implications for Rehabilitation," *The Impact of Labor Market and Health Care Economics Upon The Rehabilitation of the Injured/Disabled Worker* (East Lansing: Michigan State University, 1986).   **41**

years. Within the next ten years they are expected to increase to almost $90 billion dollars.[5] By 1995 they are expected to consume 12 percent of the gross national product.[6]

Costs Associated with the Graying of America

In terms of what motivates corporate concern with health and illness, one of the premier driving forces is clearly the graying of America. Health care experts expect the growth in the elderly population by 1995 to affect the health care system more than any other single issue. As the twentieth century makes way for the twenty-first, we will become a society in which it will be common to have four living generations in the same family, with two generations in retirement, on social security and Medicare, and often in the hospital. In the year 2010 the first "Baby Boomers" will reach the age of 65 and the postwar "Baby Boom" will result in a "Senior Boom." America's older population is itself aging: the over-65 age group (the *young* old) are growing at twice the rate of those under 65; and the over-85 age group (the *old* old) are growing at four times the rate of those under 65.

In 1960 the average American corporation had somewhere between 10 and 15 employees for each retiree, but this "support" ratio is quickly approaching a national average of 3 to 1. For the health care system, this means fewer of the low-cost, low-intensity users of medical services, and many more high-cost, high-intensity consumers. Even such a "young" firm as Federal Express, which in 1986 had 35,000 active employers and 7 retirees, has expressed concern over the costs associated with the future growth of their retiree population.

The growth in the population of older workers and retirees would be of minor concern to employers if that population remained healthy. Statistics confirm, however, that chronic health conditions and other illnesses are much more prevalent among middle-aged and older persons. There are many conditions that normally increase substantially with age: arthritis, hypertensive disease, hearing impairment, heart conditions, arteriosclerosis, and diabetes, for example. Thus, due to the correlation between age and illness, the aging phenomenon will substantially increase the cost of health care—half of which is provided via employer-sponsored health and disability benefits.

---

[5]   Tom Johnson, "Workers' Compensation: A 'Cesspool'?" *Risk Management* [1988]: 14-16.
[6]   Arthur Anderson & Co., *The Future of Healthcare: Changes and Choices* (Chicago: Arthur Anderson & Co. and The American College of Healthcare Executives, 1987).

Costs Associated with the Changing Pattern of Disability

While age is a major contributing factor to the increasing cost of health care services, it should be noted that much of the growth in the number of persons with severe disabilities has occurred among individuals ages 17 to 44. In fact, since 1962 the number of severely disabled persons 17 to 44 has risen 400 percent.[7]

Costs Associated with the Miracles of Modern Medicine

Another trend that has aggravated the costs of health care, disability and workers' compensation to both employers and the government is inspired, paradoxically, by the miracles of modern medical treatment and technology. Technologies such as CAT scans, MRIs, laser beam surgery, and nuclear medicine are available and are costly. These factors plus such modern miracles as open heart surgery and organ transplants and trauma techniques that permit the survival of individuals who have experienced serious head or spinal cord injuries or severe burns have made almost everyone a candidate for chronic illness and rehabilitation.

The aging of the population, the resultant increase in the number of people with chronic health conditions and disabilities, and the availability of high-cost medical technology have conspired to drive health care costs to unprecedented levels.

DISABILITY MANAGEMENT:
CRITICAL PRINCIPLES AND COMPONENTS

The Washington Business Group on Health is convinced that one way to control the cost of health care, workers' compensation, and disability benefits is through disability management. The concept is really quite simple: The sooner a chronically ill, injured or disabled employee recovers and returns to a productive work role, the greater the benefit to the worker, the employer, and the insurer. The employer has a choice: either choose to underwrite disability management in order to minimize the ultimate financial outlay and eliminate it entirely when the employee returns to work *or* bear the ongoing costs of supporting injured and disabled employees. The wise choice seems apparent.

---

[7]   Gerben DeJong, "Number of Adults with Severe Disabilities Has Grown," *Business and Health* (Vol. 4, No. 5 (March 1987): 22).

Workers' Compensation Strategies

A disability management orientation emphasizes:

- the early identification of job-disability problems;

- prompt medical care;

- directed and coordinated rehabilitation services;

- a willingness to modify jobs and make necessary workplace accommodations; and

- the establishment of coordinated human resource and benefit policies that facilitate work return rather than premature and unnecessary disability retirement.

It is important to recognize that to delay rehabilitation is to jeopardize rehabilitation. Both early intervention and the cooperation of all the primary parties—disabled employees, employers and providers of rehabilitation services—provide the key to successful rehabilitation and return to work. Early intervention is essential to encouraging employees to participate actively in the rehabilitation process and to preventing injuries and disabilities from resulting in disability retirement. All too often, though, rehabilitation services are delayed or absent, and as the employee's health status becomes increasingly fragile, he or she begins to accept the "sick role." Then disability benefits become an attractive alternative to continued, but problematic, employment.

The Collection and Analysis of Data

We at the Institute for Rehabilitation and Disability Management of the Washington Business Group on Health are involved in assessing the disability management and rehabilitation programs of several Fortune 500 companies, including American Airlines, Chrysler Corporation, Proctor and Gamble, AT&T, Federal Express, and ALCOA, among others. This research has provided us a remarkable opportunity to study and to learn from successful, truly excellent companies.

Every company we have visited was interested in improving their capacity to collect and analyze disability data. It was as if they all felt like Chairman Arthur Burns of Ryder Trucks, who said, "The secret lies in gathering information that exists at our fingertips—and putting it to work for us. To Ryder Systems, claims data represent an opportunity to understand costs so that we can control them." Their program succeeded in saving them more than $3 million during 1986.

One of Chrysler Corporation's first initiatives in gaining control of their health and disability costs was to retain Health Data Institute (HDI) to make a meticulous study of thousands of health-related transactions over a 30-month period. Computer analysis revealed a level of unnecessary care, inefficient practices, overutilization, fraud, and abuse that appalled Lee Iacocca and all of Chrysler management. Once the analysis was completed and studied, HDI put its computer-based system called "workability" into gear at Chrysler. This system links diagnosis-based clinical protocols with employee characteristics and job requirements to set disability-duration guidelines and to suggest appropriate care. In the first year following its adoption of "workability," Chrysler achieved a $48 million savings in health care costs!

Thus, it is clear that just as data are essential to modern management's achievement of performance objectives, so is an integrated database upon which a pragmatic and effective program of disability management may be based. Important data to include in a comprehensive disability database are information on (1) the company's current disability costs and projected claims over the predictable lifespan of its employees; (2) morbidity and absenteeism rates; (3) hospital-utilization rates; and (4) mortality trends.

Prevention, Wellness and Physical Fitness Programs

The changing nature of our society's perception of illness, from infectious disease to lifestyle-related disorders, and the growing understanding of the connection between employee health and corporate productivity are primarily responsible for the growth of worksite wellness and fitness programs. The most revolutionary and promising approach to health and compensation cost containment clearly focuses on keeping employees healthy, rather than simply paying for their care after they are sick or injured.

Companies with carefully developed corporate values and human resource strategies see their employees as an appreciating asset and thus tend to provide those opportunities and services needed to protect and foster the potential of every employee. These opportunities and services include ergonomically designed jobs, the promotion of healthy lifestyles, the early identification of health difficulties, and aroused safety programs, all of which can help reduce the incidence of illness and injury and thus lower the costs associated with disability.

By utilizing the principles of ergonomics, employers have redesigned jobs, work environments, work stations, and equipment. Ergonomists have helped many employers to reduce both the number of injuries and the discomfort at the job, to lower the rate of error and scrap, to improve employee morale, and to reduce absenteeism and employee turnover.

Physical therapy has been brought into the medical departments of many companies, while Walbro has gone one step further: it has contracted for the services of athletic trainers for pre-surgery conditioning and post-surgery recovery and work hardening. (See "Healthletics Program℠" in this book.)

Health promotion and fitness programs—although traditionally developed primarily for the able-bodied—can also benefit injured and disabled employees. A variety of firms have found that it pays to offer comprehensive programs that link health promotion and disability management. The Adolph Coors Company is one: it offers a unified disability management program that incorporates medical and rehabilitation services, counseling services, and wellness activities to encourage healthy lifestyles. After all, nutritious food, smoking cessation, stress management, and weight control are as important—if not more so—to injured and disabled persons as they are to all others.

Coordination of Services and Benefits

There is a strong corporate trend toward using case management to control health care costs. Case management generally involves three interrelated functions. The first is a multidisciplinary assessment of the disability situation that includes medical, financial, social, environmental, psychological, employment, and educational components of the problem. The second is the coordination of the procurement of services and benefits. The third is monitoring the provision of services and benefits to ensure that they (1) are appropriate, (2) can be modified to meet changing needs, (3) meet high standards of quality, and (4) are delivered in the most cost-effective way possible.

Whether one utilizes in-house staff or contracts for the service, the cardinal rule of case management is to maintain consistent contact with injured and disabled employees and all health care providers. Case management can facilitate the employee's passage through the maze of providers while assisting all concerned in making critical decisions.

Omark Industries, a manufacturer of lumber industry tools in Oregon, assigns the case management function to their industrial nurses. Within 24 hours of an injury, on or off the job, the nurse assigned contacts the employee, the supervisor, and the treating physician. It is the nurse's responsibility to coordinate all treatment and rehabilitation efforts—all toward the objective of efficient, effective care and early return to work.

Case management may be used differently in different companies, but it has the best chance of being effective under three conditions:

- If the employee population is at significant risk of becoming a high user of expensive care (premature babies, nursing home referrals);

- If the providers are self-insured, thereby at greater direct financial risk; and

- If the case management program emphasizes long-term rather than quick-fix care.

Medical Cost Management in Workers' Compensation

"The principle cause of the inflationary trend that continues to plague workers' compensation," according to David Appel and Kevin Ryan, "is the persistent inflation of medical costs which have increased at the rate of 8 percent a year since 1981."[8] In the ten-year period between 1976 and 1986, California employers saw a 300 percent increase in medical costs involving injured workers, roughly three times the rate of increase for their other medical expenses. Yet efforts to control these spiraling costs consist of little more than infrequent audits of hospital bills and physician charges.

Health consultants Polankoff and O'Rourke remind us that medical care sponsored by workers' compensation programs is provided on the traditional fee-for-service basis with usual, customary and reasonable fees for physicians and reimbursement at cost to hospitals.[9] For all practical purposes medical care provided via workers' compensation remains one of the few areas of health care which is largely unmanaged (no prepaid capitation, no negotiated rates, no utilization review, no copayments). It should not be surprising to find that hospitals, physicians and other health care providers find workers' compensation a most attractive payment system.

Good medical cost management might include such techniques as disability certification and recertification and the use of independent medical examiners. It might also include disability duration guidelines, preferred-provider arrangements, and systematic reviews of hospital and physician charges. Again, employers have alternatives: they might assign such functions to in-house staff or they might contract for such services. In either case, medical cost management is important if the employer is to be an informed purchaser of health care.

---

[8] David Appel and Kevin M. Ryan, "A Forecast for Workers' Compensation," *Digest*, Vol. 2, Issue 4: 1-11.
[9] Philip L. Polankoff and Paul F. O'Rourke, "Managed Care Applications for Workers' Compensation, *Business and Health*, Vol. 4, No.5 (March 1987): 26-27.

Fraud Investigation

Joseph Califano, in his recent book *America's Health Care Revolution,* reminds us that a "wide-open, unmanaged system simply invites fraud." Chrysler discovered that. Working with the FBI in an investigation, they uncovered practitioners who were improperly certifying worker illnesses. One chiropractor, for example, confessed to selling fake injury reports on behalf of 1,895 auto workers who illegally collected $1.5 million in disability insurance payments. Other practitioners were overprescribing drugs, which frequently found their way into street traffic.

Any fraud-prevention program should begin with a vulnerability analysis. That will highlight where the company is vulnerable and lead both the investigation of past abuse and plans for future prevention.

TRENDS AND INNOVATIONS

Over the last five years research at many institutions has focused on the status of disability management. In the course of this work, trends have been identified in firms representing a wide variety of industries across the country. It is interesting to note that the firms that have been most aggressive in the development of disability-management strategies are those that have been trendsetters in the general area of health care cost containment.

1. Employers are becoming more aware of the true cost of disability. Thus, although they may not be particularly knowledgeable about medical rehabilitation, they are beginning to recognize that while the initial cost of comprehensive rehabilitation care at specialized centers may be high, the quality of such care and the results achieved in terms of enhanced independence and continued employment may more than justify the costs.

2. They recognize that top management support is absolutely essential to successful implementation of a disability management program, but they are also aware that the major players in such implementation are their front-line supervisors and managers. Thus, providing training and support services to these supervisors is also crucial.

3. Companies with successful return-to-work programs report that union participation is a key component in developing positive disability management strategies, and that unions and management

can work together constructively in several areas to encourage job retention.

4. Firms are beginning to appreciate that successful disability management, rehabilitation and return-to-work efforts require well defined and coordinated human resource, benefit, and general management policies which support the return-to-work objectives. Workers' compensation and equal employment opportunity personnel can frequently provide considerable assistance to other departments in the design, development, and review of disability policies and practices. In fact such "technology transfer" is often advocated by consultants.

5. Employers are beginning to assign someone within the company the central responsibility for developing and coordinating disability management activities. They recognize that successful disability management programs require a willingness to consider creative options and flexibility to facilitate the return to work (such options as flexible hours and work assignments, light duty, and transitional work). They are beginning to utilize employee assistance programs as a resource in this effort.

6. Charging workers' compensation costs back to the employee's department or business unit is becoming a common practice because it serves as a powerful incentive both to manage disability and to return injured employees to work. Employers are also making a concerted effort to educate treating physicians who usually are not well informed about the tasks associated with specific jobs. Evidence clearly indicates that treating physicians often feel ill-equipped in terms of determining the injured worker's readiness to return to work. Most respond favorably to outreach and education by employers.

7. Companies are also becoming much more knowledgeable about how to select and monitor private rehabilitation firms. Weyerhaeuser, for example, utilizes a request-for-proposal approach. They train providers to the specific needs and requirements of their company. They meticulously check references and manage the provision of care by requiring timely documentation and pre-approvals.

8. Employers are also beginning to utilize physical therapy services for purposes of prevention, employee screening, gradual conditioning for return to work, and rehabilitation. They use a variety of arrangements including contracts with private providers, the employment of physical therapists by the firm (much as they would

employ nurses), and traditional reimbursement for hospital-based physical therapy.

9. Finally, in terms of managing disability, rehabilitation and return-to-work, employers are beginning to make less of a distinction between employees who become disabled on the job and those who become disabled off the job.

OBSTACLES AND ISSUES CONFRONTING EMPLOYERS

It is important to recognize that there are several major obstacles that frustrate the best of corporate intentions. First, there have been serious questions raised by employers and insurers about the quality and costs of rehabilitation services provided to injured workers. Looking into the status of disability management is enough to convince almost everyone of the paucity of cost-effective data that could convince corporate America of the wisdom and value of the rehabilitation investment. Many employers are understandably skeptical about the payoff of rehabilitation and are thus not staunchly committed to it.

Several of the trendsetters (3M, AT&T, Weyerhaeuser, and ALCOA) have not in fact been driven by "bottom line" questions. They have adopted the disability management strategy largely on the basis of their commitment to their employees and their overall corporate culture.

The disability management story would be incomplete without notation of several other issues as well. Problems attached to economic downturns, reductions in work force, takeovers, and mergers have affected the majority of American corporations sometime during the last five years. These problems affect disability management prospects in several ways. First, such firms frequently do not have jobs for injured workers to return to. Second, such economic dislocation promotes extreme stress in the work force. Third, there is clear evidence that in the face of layoffs and plant closures, at least, the disability and workers' compensation application rates soar as workers look for some economic haven in the storm.

Employers across the country are rightfully concerned about the growing evidence of disability and workers' compensation claims based on stress and other mental health conditions including depression.[10] In the case of disability benefits, such coverage is extended to dependents; thus the patient in question may be the employee's teenage son or daughter, spouse, or in some cases an elderly parent who is dependent upon the wage earner.

___
[10]   *Newsweek,* April 25, 1988.

Other conditions also cause concern. Alcohol and drug abuse continues to be a major and growing problem for many employers. As a disability and as a serious chronic and terminal condition, AIDS is bound to have a profound impact upon employer health care costs. Yet most firms have not yet even established an AIDS policy.

In addition, even the most progressive companies admit that the disability benefit and workers' compensation route is unfortunately being used all too often to "retire" employees who are regarded as troublesome. While senior corporate officials may deplore this practice as counter to both company philosophy and good management procedure, on the plant floor and in the office where the supervisor must deal with such individuals on a day-to-day basis, disability and injury are sometimes seen as a solution to a thorny personnel problem.

CONCLUSION

Frank Bowe, a leading advocate of disability rights, reminds us that employers who adopt the disability management strategy—those who offer early intervention, rehabilitation, and return to work to their injured or disabled employees—are providing assistance potentially far more valuable to their employees than direct financial benefits and compensation.[11] He argues that the rush to disability retirement reflects misguided compassion at best and, at worst, the ill-founded belief that the worker who has suffered a chronic illness, serious injury or disability is of limited value to the firm.

In the final analysis, much of this issue is a matter of attitudes and values. One consultant active in this area has said, "Disability is an attitude issue, not just an income issue, not even a health or medical issue. Investment in disability management should not be perceived as an added cost—rather it should be seen as a positive investment." Simply put, disability management is one way to reduce the inherent costs of disability and workers' compensation while promoting independence, the realization of human potential, and economic productivity.

---

[11]   Frank Bowe, *Coming Back: Directions for Rehabilitation and Disabled Workers* (Fayetteville: University of Arkansas, 1986).

SUGGESTED READINGS

Akabas, Sheila, "Disability Management: A Longstanding Trade Union Mission with Some New Initiatives," *Journal of Applied Rehabilitation Counseling,* Vol. 17, No. 3 (Fall 1986):33-36.

Anderson, Arthur, & Co. and The American College of Healthcare Executives, *The Future of Healthcare: Changes and Choices* (Chicago: Arthur Anderson, 1987).

Appel, David and Kevin M.Ryan, "A Forecast for Workers' Compensation," *Digest,* Vol 2, No. 4 (Dec. 1987): 1-11.

Bowe, Frank, *Coming Back: Directions for Rehabilitation and Disabled Workers* (Fayetteville: University of Arkansas, 1986).

Califano, John A., Jr., *America's Health Care Revolution, Who Lives? Who Dies? Who Pays?* (New York: Random House, 1986).

Carbine, Michael E. and Gail E. Schwartz, *Strategies for Managing Disability Costs* (Washington, D.C.: Washington Business Group on Health, 1987).

Carpenter, Eugenia S., "Roadblocks to Rehabilitation," *Business and Health,* Vol. 3, No. 2 (December 1985): 22-24.

DeJong, Gerben, "Number of Adults with Severe Disabilities Has Grown," *Business and Health,* Vol. 4, No. 5 (March 1987): 22.

Eckenhoff, Edward A., "Medical Rehabilitation for Disabled Employees," *Business and Health,* Vol. 1, No. 6 (May 1984): 29-31.

"The Enemy Within," *Time* (September 15, 1986): 58-68.

Galvin, Donald E. "Employer Based Disability Management and Rehabilitation Programs," *Annual Review of Rehabilitation* (New York: Springer Publishing, 1986).

Galvin, Donald E., "Health Promotion, Disability Management and Rehabilitation in the Workplace," *Rehabilitation Literature,* Vol. 47, Nos. 9-10 (September-October, 1986): 218-23.

Galvin, Donald E., "Labor Market Economics: Implications for Rehabilitation," in Gleason, Sandra E., Eugenia S. Carpenter, Hillary A. Murt, and Donald E. Galvin, *The Impact of Labor Market and Health Care Economics upon the Rehabilitation of the Injured/Disabled Worker* (East Lansing: Michigan State University, 1986).

Galvin, Donald E., Denise G. Tate, and Gail E. Schwartz, "Disability Management Research: Current Status, Needs and Implications for Study," *Journal of Applied Rehabilitation*, Vol. 17, No. 3 (Fall 1986): 43-48.

Goldbeck, Willis, "Introduction: Strategies for Managing Disability Costs," in Carbine and Schwartz, *Strategies for Managies Disability Costs*.

Iacocca, Lee (with L. Novak), *Iacocca: An Autobiography* (New York: New Bantam Books, 1984).

Johnson, Tom, "Workers' Compensation a 'Cesspool'?" *Risk Management* (1988): 14-16.

Lundell, Paula M., "Disability: A Manageable Risk," *Health Cost Management*, Vol. 2, No. 2 (March-April 1985): 5-12.

Merrill, Jeffrey C., "Defining Case Management," *Business and Health*, Vol. 2, No. 8 (July-August 1985): 5-9.

Milstein, Arnold, Gail Nethercut, and Michael Martin, "Controlling Medical Costs in Workers' Compensation," *Business and Health*, Vol. 5, No. 5 (March 1988): 34-36.

Mitchell, Kenneth, D. and Donald E. Shrey, "The Risk Manager's Guide to Disability Management," *Risk Management* (September 1985): 42-46.

Polankoff, Philip L. and Paul F. O'Rourke, "Managed Care Applications for Workers' Compensation," *Business and Health*, Vol. 4, No. 5 (March 1987):26-27.

_____"Workers' Compensation—Managing the Cost Crunch," *Risk Management* (1988): 52-53.

Reich, Robert B., *The Next American Frontier: A Provocative Program for Economic Renewal* (New York: Penguin Books, 1983).

Schwartz, Gail E., "Disability Cost: The Impending Crisis," *Business and Health*, Vol. 1, No.5 (May 1984): 27-29.

_____"State of the Art: Corporate Behavior in Disability Management Survey Results" (Washington, D.C.: Washington Business Group on Health, 1986).

"Stress on the Job," *Newsweek* (April 25, 1988): 40-45.

Thurow, Lester C., "Medicine vs. Economics," *New England Journal of Medicine*, Vol. 313, No. 10 (1983): 611-13.

Tonti, Don G., Tamara Trudeau, and Martin Daniel, "Linking Fitness Activities to Rehabilitation," *Business and Health* (September 1987): 23-27.

Wilber, Curtis, "Rehabilitating Workers: Where Does Health Promotion Fit In? Employee Health and Fitness," *Health and Well Being,* Vol. 10, No. 1 (January 1988): 1-5.

Specific Reports (Prepared by the general staff of the Institute for Rehabilitation and Disability Management of the Washington Business Group on Health):

"ALCOA: A Case Study" (1987).

"Federal Express: A Case Study (1987).

"Health Management and Physical Therapy: A Review of the Literature" (1987).

"Weyerhaeuser: A Case Study" (1987).

PART TWO

Three Success Stories

4

A Corporate Safety and Health Program: The First Line of Defense

Martha H. Miller

The issue of workers' compensation cost containment has been a political football for a number of years. Employers cry out that costs are too high and question the work ethic of employees. Injured employees often feel their needs and rights are ignored. Meanwhile, entrepreneurs gear up to provide both the employers and the injured workers with their services. Is there a way out of this lose-lose scenario?

I propose to you that there is! A way out of allegations, claims, counterclaims, lost productivity, and employee suffering. There is an effective cost containment strategy for compensable injuries that can satisfy all parties—a corporate safety and health program. Such a program has proved to be a first-rate management tool for decreasing injuries, suffering, cost, and dissatisfaction.

Let's discuss the difference between a safety and health program, on the one hand, and a successful safety and health program, on the other. To have a successful program, certain components are essential (See Diagram 1.).

Diagram 1.

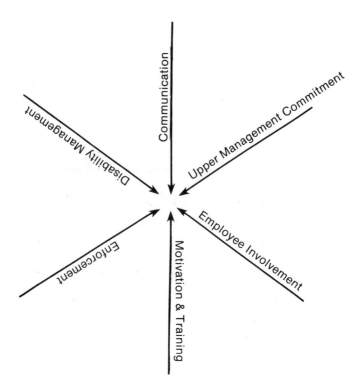

UPPER MANAGEMENT COMMITMENT

The reason that upper management commitment is essential is that without it, the employees will not believe in the system. This was a finding on a recent survey conducted by DuPont Safety Services. That survey identified upper management commitment as the first of three key factors that led to a successful program.

How can one identify upper management commitment? One must find evidence in four distinct areas (See Diagram 2.).

To expose employees to the "corporate culture" at Consumers Power Company, certain specific steps are taken, which are designed to assure that new, as well as existing, employees are well aware of the company's stance on safety in the workplace. First, the new employee orientation includes a section on safety rules, practices, and procedures. Second, all employees are provided with a pocket-size "Accident Prevention Manual."

Diagram 2.

Corporate Culture	Staffing
Funding	Accountability

The cover page of the manual contains a statement from the president of the company, which reads:

> "Adequate attention to safety is a condition of employment for all employees of Consumers Power Company, without exception."

At the beginning of each calendar year, employees are involved in safety kick-off activities. There is also a videotape from the president and CEO reviewing the past year's accident history, with a focus on the safety goals of the new year.

Many of the areas sponsor a family safety night. Family members tour the facilities, ride in bucket trucks, and receive safety-related instruction, such as CPR, home fire safety, and vacation safety tips. Our employees frequently receive state and national awards for saving lives, and these lifesaving skills have usually been learned at their work headquarters. In fact, employees have become as accustomed to winning national awards as they are to winning in-house awards for an accident-free time period.

On a quarterly basis, Consumers Power holds a senior management review of recordable lost-time accidents. The applicable officer presents the facts of each case to the company president and his senior staff. The emphasis is on the action taken to prevent recurrence.

The safety of employees and the general public is part and parcel of corporate objectives, strategies and policies of this company and is, in my opinion, closely interwoven into the corporate culture.

A second indicator of management commitment to a health and safety program is its willingness to staff the corporate safety and health department adequately. As the role of the safety and health professional becomes more complex, many specialties are required to address safety and health problems and adequate staffing requirements increase. Industrial hygienists, industrial engineers, and medical personnel all support the cause.

Including accountability for safety performance is another sign of management's commitment to its health and safety program. Employees and all levels of management have a share of the responsibility of assuring the success of the corporate safety and health program. Many companies rate employees during their performance appraisal as to how safely they perform their jobs and to their general attitude toward safety. Some companies deny or reduce pay raises for supervisors whose employees demonstrate poor safety performance. A few years ago, a Consumers Power Company executive vice-president informed his staff that if they couldn't manage safety, they couldn't manage anything. That's accountability! I might add that he got the results he was seeking.

To ascertain a company's commitment to its health and safety program, one must only look at its funding: Does it appear to want to pay for the ounce of prevention or the pound of cure? National Safety Council statistics for 1986 state that the cost per disabling injury was $12,600. How many disabling injuries occurred in your business in 1986? How many dollars were budgeted for prevention? Where was your priority—prevention or cure? To a certain degree, the choice is clearly ours.

How can one obtain management commitment? Frequently the quickest route is through use of these approaches: cost data, employee relations concern, or public relations concern.

Cost data can be presented in many different ways:

- Cost per accident
- Medical costs
- Cost per year
- Equipment costs
- Cost per lost manhour
- Rehabilitation costs

It is always helpful to compare your costs to other businesses that perform similar functions, utility to utility, for example. Such comparisons are available for a variety of industries through the National Safety Council.

Employee relations are always important. Employees are very quick to point out inconsistencies between written safety and health policies and actual practice. Such concerns need to be addressed promptly. Delayed responses could lead employees to conclude that management does not care, or worse yet, that management has something to hide. Frequent visits by MIOSHA inspectors should be a triggering mechanism to address employee concerns immediately.

Public relations are also an important measure of company concern. The general public is our neighbor. Their trust in our ability to conduct our business in a manner that does not endanger their health and safety or the health and safety of their descendants should be a given. However, that is not always the case. Many times the public brings to the surface concerns that require a change in the way we do business.

EMPLOYEE INVOLVEMENT

The second component essential to a successful safety and health program is employee involvement. We hear a lot these days about such involvement mechanisms as job ownership, participative management, and quality circles. The employee is obviously the person who should be most concerned about his or her own safety. After all, the employee is the one who bleeds, feels the pain, and frequently ends up with altered relationships and lifestyles.

Historically, management has resisted employees seeking input into the safety programs. Some employees, on the other hand, have taken the stance that management has full responsibility for protecting them. Currently, logic and reason appear to be making headway. Many companies and unions have developed agreements that allow labor and management to work together toward a safer work environment.

Joint programs have the potential to be effective weapons in the battle against work-related illnesses and injuries. In 1983, Consumers Power Company and the Utility Worker's Union of America negotiated a joint union-management local safety committee agreement. Since we have headquarters located throughout the state of Michigan, the agreement provides for many local committees. It also identifies the scope and membership of the committees.

Employee involvement also means the involvement of the supervisor. To the employee, the supervisor is the company. If the supervisor ignores safety rules and condones unsafe practices, the employee assumes that is the way the company wants it. Unfortunately the average employee does not see the company as a whole—a fact which brings us back to accountability.

MOTIVATION AND TRAINING

The third component of a successful program is motivation and training. Even those of us charged with developing and administering corporate programs occasionally become complacent. Employees are no different. To keep us all at a high level of alertness it is necessary to vary the types and methods of stimulation provided. Safety meetings and safety-related training should be designed and developed both to assure a high level of employee interest and to bring about desired behavior.

Employees need quality training if they are to do their jobs efficiently and safely. Safety needs to be incorporated into the how, what, and where of every task. A job safety analysis is one means of helping the employee identify the various actions, tools, and hazards contained in a given job.

Training in the proper use of tools, protective equipment, and work procedures and clear explanation of safety rules are further reflections of management's commitment to the safety concept. But training should go beyond instruction in how to do a specific job safely. A saturation concept eventually instills an *awareness* of safe work habits at work and at home.

ENFORCEMENT

Enforcement of safety rules is the fourth component, one commonly identified as always needed but frequently lacking. Suppose an employee is injured due to a violation of safety rules. Has he or she already been disciplined by the injury? Or should discipline in the form of time off the job, written letter, or verbal warning also be issued? Whatever answer you choose, consistency is crucial. Employees are keenly attuned to disparate treatment. In addition, if discipline is to bring about the desired change in behavior, timeliness is essential. In my opinion, discipline that occurs many months after the incident creates employee relations problems. The delay in discipline may also contribute to a delay in the employee's return to work. Occasionally, employees develop subjective complaints to delay returning to the workplace, and this occurs more frequently if they know they will face discipline upon their return.

What do you do with the employee who violates but is not injured? The supervisor who condones or actually supports rule violations? All of these issues could be dealt with in advance with a corporate safety and health program.

DISABILITY MANAGEMENT

Once an injury has occurred, aggressive medical case management and progressive return-to-work policies will enhance and support an employee's return to work. A focus on ability, not disability, will allow an employee to return on limited duty. Early return to work is in the best interest of both the employer and the employee.

At Consumers Power Company we have changed our return-to-work policies to treat off-the-job illnesses and injuries the same as work-related illnesses and injuries. This change in policy has helped defuse employee complaints that only work-related restrictions are accommodated. Both sides benefit: employees are able to preserve sick leave and the company reduces absenteeism.

COMMUNICATION

Let's look at the communication component. I consider this component the key to every other major component. The purpose of communication is to inform, influence, and motivate. The program essentials mentioned earlier must all be communicated in order to bring about the change we are all seeking.

You have probably noticed that in this discussion I have not given much time to the usual safety areas of inspection, guarding, protective equipment, and so forth. I did so purposely. In my opinion, inspecting, guarding, and equipping will not prevent accidents and disability unless upper management commitment, employee involvement, motivation, training and enforcement are present. You have to have upper management commitment. You have to have employee involvement. You have to have motivation and training, enforcement, and disability management. Without those you cannot have a fully effective program.

Employees do not have to be injured. Prevention is the key to reduced suffering and cost containment. A well-designed corporate safety and health program can be the first line of defense.

5

Commitment at Steelcase

James C. Soule

Sometime over three years ago I came to Steelcase from the world of consulting to become Steelcase's Vice President of Human Resources. Now the world of consulting was a comparatively quiet world: we only dealt with things like mergers and takeovers and board revolutions. No workers' compensation. Since I've come to be part of Steelcase, however, workers' comp has changed my life.

Let me explain what I mean. From October thru mid-December I put about 3,000 miles on my car, primarily from talking with people from business and labor about workers' comp. As part of the "Economic Alliance," I was helping take a look at reshaping the law. Now, people I don't even know don't like me because of my part in the Economic Alliance's approach to workers' compensation. Reporters from *Crain's Business, Grand Rapids Press, Detroit News,* and *Detroit Free Press* have all asked my opinion on workers' comp, which is a subject that technically I don't know a heck of a lot about. I'm not particularly comfortable talking about things I don't know a lot about, and I particularly don't like having the words I say interpreted in a way I don't think I said; but that's another matter.

Yesterday we had a case in workers' compensation court. I wound up spending all day in a very small room in the state office building in Grand Rapids with about 18 people. At the end we got adjourned for about six weeks. Near as I can figure, based both on the schedule that's gone on and on, what we have to talk about, and witnesses who have to come up, we may be done by Thanksgiving. And again, the topic is workers' comp.

Today I drove to Lansing and Friday I drive to Detroit, again for meetings on workers' comp. I've come to hate words beginning with "w."

So I'm not really going to talk about workers' comp per se. I'm going to talk about Steelcase; that begins with an "s." I'm going to talk about our company and about our commitment to our people, and I think that workers' comp will kind of fall into place as we go along.

COMPANY PHILOSOPHY

When I use the term "us" to speak about Steelcase, I really mean "us"— all of us at Steelcase. Our company philosophy talks about all of the people groups the company seeks to serve. We talk about our employees, our shareholders, our dealers, our customers, and our vendors. It really says that we are committed to excellence as we deal with all of these groups, and that no one group's interests will be put above the rest. We won't put any individual above any of the others.

Our company philosophy goes on to say that we don't consider profit a dirty word; that we're really in business to make money; and that we WILL make a profit and we will share that profit with our employees, with our vendors, with our customers, and with our dealers as we go along doing business. Our employees, as we look at it, are really an asset to us, an asset to be managed very, very carefully, not just in terms of what they're doing in their work but all across the board. We manage our employees as we would any precious asset—money, diamonds, whatever it might happen to be.

We do this by encouraging participation in very real terms and by putting ourselves, as management, on the line. For example, we have in each of our plants employee relations people whose sole function is to act as employee advocates to deal with such issues as discipline, job change, company policy, and other more personal matters. We also have a safety engineer in each plant, to deal with all aspects of safety issues. These are expensive people to keep in place, but it's part of our commitment to our company and to our employees.

We have an open door policy. What this means is that any employee who wants to talk with any member of senior management about anything, can. And they often do and it's liable to be about anything they want to talk about. I see this as an ongoing attitude survey, and I wind up learning a lot about how we're doing as management in many different areas, one of which is dealing with injured employees. It keeps everybody honest. It also keeps everybody involved in what's going on .

As an organization, we also have an extreme commitment to safety. We have one safety engineer per plant, and we do all kinds of training. Each foreman has a weekly safety meeting with all of his or her employees. We have an industrial hygiene group. We have an environmental hygiene group. We set annual safety goals with each plant manager. (Actually, this is one of things that gets me. Say we have a goal, for example, of six serious injuries. As we come to the end of the year and we've only had five, I'm always wondering who's going to be picked to be injured so we can hit the goal. So I'm trying to get somebody to reword that thing.)

Progress toward the goals is reviewed at least semi-annually in a general meeting, which includes all manufacturing management and me, as vice-president of human resources. Awards are given, first, to the safest plant and then to the one that showed the most improvement in safety over the previous year. We regularly post signs indicating the number of manhours worked since the last lost-time injury and the last serious injury. We investigate each injury very thoroughly, and we publish the results to all members of management, not just plant management.

Based on our own internal research into injuries and their causes, we're beginning to do a lot of job redesign. Our tendency is to look at injuries as something we can prevent, and job redesign fits into that notion.

We have a disciplinary point system for violations of company policy. I won't explain this in depth, but if you earn 160 points over a period of time, you wind up getting fired. (I should have mentioned that we are not a union plant.) We may bring you back eventually, for a variety of reasons, but you tend to get fired and subjected to all sorts of horrible things.

One of the reasons I mention this is that among the infractions assigned the highest points are safety violations: hands in die gets you 100-120 points, which gets you close to being out the door. Unsafe hi-lo driving, horseplay, hitting your foreman and meaning it. (Just casually hitting your foreman is okay; but if you mean it, that's a lot of points.) We're really committed to that kind of a safety program because we're committed to our people, and we see that kind of commitment and safety going hand in hand.

But we're not just committed to the healthy worker. We're also committed to the worker who by happenstance gets injured or becomes restricted   **67** for whatever reason. Our policy is to keep injured workers working whenever possible. Just stop and think about it: If you replace an experienced worker with an inexperienced one because your experienced worker has been sent home, it costs you money in lost efficiency. Plus you wind up having to find an extra worker and pay for medical expenses. Also, keeping somebody home costs money. Since we share profits with our employees, keeping an employee home not only costs the company money; it costs me money personally. And my wallet is important to me!

RESTRICTED WORK

One of the key jobs of our employee relations managers, whom I mentioned earlier, is to seek out work for injured or restricted employees who cannot work their regular jobs, for whatever reason. We want to get them back to work. We want to have them working productively because we recognize that that's important to their morale, their self-esteem, and their families. We even wind up putting people from the factory to work in the office if we can't find other light duty work for them. Last year in our Compensation and Benefits Department, for example, we used restricted employees for about 5,500 hours of work. In most cases they did simple filing, but some were able to do claims processing once we trained them. We found that we were then able to release other office workers to do more specialized work. It was a nice closed system, which worked very well for everyone.

We are also trying a different track. We have established a Materials Reprocessing Department, created as a transitional workplace to try to get people moving from injury back to full production, full work. This is essentially an organization within one of the plants at Steelcase that is oriented toward the transition time experienced by injured workers. This department provides a variety of operations—all light duty work— that injured employees can do. For example, we use a lot of gloves in the manufacturing process. For a long time we sent our gloves out to be washed. Actually, we had an interesting phenomenon. We would buy a new batch of gloves, use them once, and send them out to be cleaned. We would get used gloves, very used gloves, back. Somebody must have been buying our gloves. Anyway, we began having our restricted employees wash our gloves in our new Materials Reprocessing Department. Without even calculating how many gloves we aren't buying because we are doing this ourselves, our net profit from this department over the first six months was $80,000.

We also have a lot of scrap—screws, nuts, bolts—that we have to sort through one way or another. Injured people can do that, and that winds up saving us money. The long and short of it is that our getting people back to that kind of an environment makes them feel a lot more positive about Steelcase. They become more committed, more loyal employees. We wind up saving money overall because we're doing services inside that otherwise we'd been doing outside. So, from all standpoints, including profit and loss, this puts us ahead of the game.

At Steelcase we like to think we have developed a partnership between our medical department and our workers' compensation department. We use our medical department to diagnose and treat the injured worker so as to enable him or her to return to work. The purpose of our workers' comp department, itself, is to ensure that when there is a claim, it is handled promptly so that our people get their money as quickly as possible. We do not look at workers' comp as a dirty word. We look at it as a benefit we want our employees to enjoy should circumstances cause them to qualify for it.

Recently we have become involved in health promotion and employee assistance programs. We have instituted a health promotion program in the workplace, called H.A.L.O., which includes a physical therapist who functions within our medical department. Basically we see this as both a cost-saving mechanism and a means of controlling the course of therapy for an injured worker. In addition, we have established an employee assistance program within our counseling center to enable us to work up front with people who have substance abuse or other similar disabilities. With our Materials Reprocessing Department and other light-duty jobs, our medical, physical therapy and employee assistance programs, and our workers' comp program, we have developed a nice complete circle to help our employee return back to full productivity as quickly as possible.

Steelcase's commitment is toward the worker—not just the healthy worker but the worker who may have become disabled—who for whatever reason has become restricted from doing the job he or she had previously been doing. And we think it really, really pays for us. Our turnover, for example, is about three times less than the national average. Once people come to us they are committed to us because we're committed to them. And that's a cost savings. Our productivity is among the highest in the nation and definitely among the highest in our industry. We think that's because of our commitment—us to our workers and our workers to us.

WORKERS' COMPENSATION

The workers' compensation system itself, at least for us, works pretty well most of the time. Occasionally we will have a dispute with a worker **69** that results in litigation. I personally experienced that for the first time yesterday, sitting in the courtroom watching how this process goes. It's interesting.

People keep telling me it's better than it used to be. I say, "Holy cow!"

Anyway, at Steelcase we try to treat any employee with the same amount of dignity 100 percent of the time, whether the employee came to us healthy and is still healthy, came to us disabled, or came to us healthy and became disabled or restricted while with us.

We see workers' compensation payments completely as a benefit for our qualified employees. Our policy has always been: when in doubt, go for the employee. But at times there are bound to be disputes or discrepancies between what the employee says and what our medical department says.

To analyze all these situations we have formed a medical review board, which is functioning very well. Our board has people from employee relations, from our medical department, from our workers' comp department, and a few extras who wander in from time to time because they like the coffee and donuts. We talk about each case in depth. We try to understand as clearly as possible what went on and whether or not this injury could in fact possibly have been caused by work at Steelcase. If we decide it was, we'll go that way; we'll go for compensation. If in our judgment, however, it wasn't, we'll try to get back to the employee and say "We don't think it was. Do you have any other evidence that you haven't presented so far?" And we'll try to work with the employee again as positively as we can.

We strongly believe that effective management of injured or restricted employees can ultimately help reduce costs. We believe this even though we recognize the cost of employee relations people and the cost of safety people and the cost of all the other things we're doing. We believe, for example, we could be way ahead if our health promotion program is successful in hitting lifestyle-related illnesses, not to mention just getting people healthy.

As we were looking into this program we call H.A.L.O., one of our researchers estimated that something like 60 percent of the workers currently handling factory jobs are not fit enough to do that work. Now, when you stop and think about that, it's amazing. I don't know where in the world that statistic came from, but if it's true or even close to true, you know we all have a workers' compensation problem. So we believe that if our H.A.L.O. program could reduce lifestyle-related problems by even 10 percent, it would pay for itself twice over each year. We'd get a six-month payback, and we don't think that's bad. Overall we see our health program as helping us to reduce our costs, increase both morale and company loyalty and therefore productivity, and decrease turnover.

We also feel that a very strong and meaningful commitment to safety is an absolutely vital and necessary part of our doing business. This commitment signals that we are committed to our people, and therefore our people wind up being committed to us.

6

An Attitude Problem

Kevin M. Meade

I was at a Self-Insurers' Association meeting about 15 months ago, primarily to hear the association's interpretation of the new workers' compensation legislation, when I met a friend standing in the lobby of the auditorium. He began to talk about some fellow who had recently been appointed by Governor Blanchard to be the director of the Bureau of Workers' Disability Compensation. He said that this fellow, who was a comp attorney, was going to talk that morning. And I went in and listened to what the new law was going to do or possibly going to be; I heard about the magistrates, the administrative law judges, and all that. And then we were introduced to Ed Welch and Ed spoke for probably 20 minutes.

He talked about the irony of his situation as a plaintiff's attorney, being in between the employer and the injured worker—which I thought was an interesting perspective. As an employer I had never tried to get in between the two. I had tried to get on top of a few of them, but never in between.

And then he digressed, I thought for a moment, into some things about attitudes and he made the observation that in his experience, a lot of the plants that he had worked with that had workers' compensation problems, and probably high cost associated with those problems, also had a lot of other employee attitude-type problems, like absenteeism, high grievance activity, and things like that. The more he talked about this, as he digressed, the more it meant to me as an individual.

So I went up to him after the meeting and told him, "Hey, I have been there before. It was almost like you were looking over my shoulder."

He had requested the opportunity to visit some plants and see what was going on in them and I invited him to come over to our plant in Ionia, which he did several months later. We toured it, had a nice conversation, and then about two or three months ago he called and asked if I would speak to a couple of people about the experience that we had had. Well, I am glad I never dealt with Ed about a couple of dollars on a settlement because his concept and my concept of "a couple" are quite different.

But let's talk about our Ionia plant. During the 1950s, when it was owned by Mitchell-Bentley out of Owosso, employment at that plant peaked at about 5,000. When my company purchased the plant in 1971 from A.O. Smith, employment had dropped to 250. Throughout the decade of the l960s there had been a radical decrease: in fact, there had not been one person hired during that decade. By 1978, when I became Industrial Relations Manager at the Ionia facility, our work force had increased again to about 1,000 people; but because of retirements and attrition due to the long layoffs I found myself dealing with a completely different work force than had been there when I started in 1973. In 1973 we had had a fairly mature work force; it was just starting to grow and expand; the people had been around for years. There was no absenteeism to speak of. Workers' compensation was something rare, left for the attorneys to deal with.

By 1978 we were dealing with it ourselves, and I saw things happening in our work force that I had seen on college campuses and university campuses in the 1960s in the student population. There was almost a literal throwing out of office of the old guard that had been in charge of the union for years. These young people were not going to be told what was important, what was significant. They were not going to be told how to run their local; they were going to run it themselves. They rallied in a volatile way around issues of safety and health and were quick to grieve those sorts of things. In short, we found we were dealing with a whole different animal than we had ever dealt with before.

My topic this morning is the effect of what we saw there and how the attitudes that Ed reflected on in his presentation impacted in Ionia. We did have employee attitude problems, plenty of them (See Figure 1). We had absenteeism, prolific grievance activity, and other problems.

I think one of the most common problems for people in charge of handling plant functions is absenteeism. The general concept is that if your employees are happy, if they are satisfied with their work, and if they are comfortable with what they are doing, they are probably going to

Figure 1.

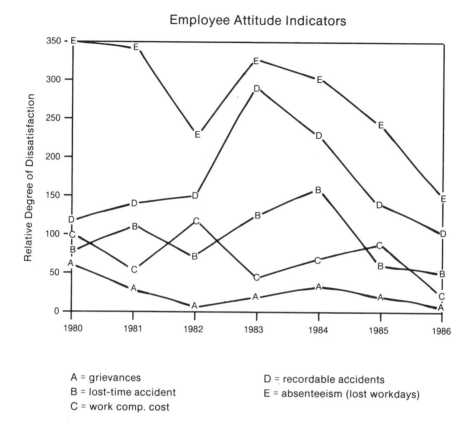

Employee Attitude Indicators

A = grievances
B = lost-time accident
C = work comp. cost

D = recordable accidents
E = absenteeism (lost workdays)

come to work most of the time. If they are not happy or they are not satisfied or they are not comfortable, they are probably not going to come to work all that frequently. I like to think that if your absentee level is less than 3 percent, your people are probably generally satisfied with you as an employer. But if your absentee level is consistently over 3 to 3.5 percent, and it was not because there was a big snow day last month or something like that, that is an indicator that there is probably some attitude problem in your work force and you ought to be looking at it.

A second measure that you can look at has to do with grievance activity. Happy workers, I think it is safe to say, probably do not file a lot of grievances. Unhappy workers, on the other hand, probably do. So if you have a plant that has a lot of grievance activity, it is probably an indication that there is an attitude problem or that there is something wrong within your work force. As an attorney Ed may not be aware of this, but as an industrial relations person, I can tell you that at the plant level there is a real tendency to blame the union for grievances. Management thinks that there are a lot of grievances because of the union, and it is easy to fall back on that theory and catch yourself in a trap. The union really

75

is not anything more than employees elected by other employees to represent their views and express their opinions and attitudes. So if you have a lot of grievance activity in your facility and those people that are filing all those grievances continue to get elected, then in reality you probably have a problem.

A third measure of employees' attitudes is outside regulatory agency activity. If you have a lot of employees calling MIOSHA, the Department of Health, the Bureau of Workers' Disability Compensation, and the civil rights agencies, or you have a lot of inspections other than routine walk-arounds, I think you can assume there is something wrong, there is some attitude problem out there. Most organizations, whether they are union or non-union, are going to set up a system to prevent outside intervention. If you have a lot of outside intervention, even as an indication that your employees' attitudes are negative, you ought to recognize that your system is not working.

IONIA IN THE LATE 1970S

At our Ionia plant in 1979 and 1980, all these measures were way out of control, far from normal. Our absenteeism ran into 8 or 9 percent a month. Our grievance activity (looking back at it I don't believe it myself) was running 700 to 800 a year. They covered every conceivable subject, and there were so many of them that you could not deal with them. We had inspections from MIOSHA and from the Department of Labor's workers' compensation people. The bureau actually sent people into our plant to sit down and talk with us and the union about why all our employees were going to them. For someone new walking into the job of plant industrial relations director, it was overwhelming. And on top of that, in early 1980 we were invaded by a corporate task force.

Part of our corporate procedures was to have each plant record, chart, and report lost-time accidents to corporate headquarters. There these data would be put on a graph and compared to that from the other plants. Our data were so far out of line with the other 20 plants in our division that they would not fit on the same scale. We could not be graphed and that got corporate attention fairly effectively! Specifically, at the end of fiscal 1979, the Ionia plant was fully responsible for 25 percent of the entire corporation's workers' compensation costs although it was only one of over 50 manufacturing facilities that General Tire and Rubber owned over the continental United States. For those of you who are associated with a company of that size, you can imagine the reaction you get when one plant generates 25 percent of the cost in anything. If it was profits, they would come and kiss us. But this was not profits; it was a loss. So we had a task force of seven people from all over the corporation descend upon us.

Funny, at the time I was furious! I felt I did not need any help, that I could do it myself. Obviously the corporation, in its infinite wisdom, felt otherwise. They sent these people in. My two predecessors had had a good answer for the corporate question: What is wrong up there in Michigan? (This is the only plant the corporation has in Michigan.) The answer they used for their five years, which had worked pretty well for them, was that Michigan has lousy comp laws and you cannot do anything about it. You go to court, but you are beaten before you get there. You do everything you can, you yell at the Chamber of Commerce, but the whole system—with the administrative law judges and the Appeal Board— is terrible and you cannot do anything about it. Michigan just has lousy comp laws.

Well, the task force showed up and I told them that. I said there is nothing we can do about it: Michigan has lousy comp laws.

They disagreed.

They spent six weeks in the plant; they interviewed anyone they wanted to, behind closed doors. They called the union representatives in one at a time and spent hours with them, asking about what was going on up here. We do not know to this day what they said. The task force interviewed us behind closed doors, too. But we were carefully enough trained that we did not spill out our guts to them. They were there to help us and we could say we were glad to have them; but we were not about to tell them anything. They interviewed employees: they went out into the plant on three shifts. In fact, we never knew when they were going to pop in or out. They had meetings with themselves in hotels and motels outside the plant. Finally, they came back with a report that said, in substance, you have an attitude problem in Ionia and you have got to deal with it.

They had looked at our lost-time accidents (remember, they were unchartable by normal standards), and they did not find a bunch of ambulances waiting outside the door to cart people out. That was not the case. The great majority of the lost-time accidents we had were one- or two-day incidents. They were what I guess you could call minor injuries. Obviously they were not minor to the injured employee, but they were not amputations. We were not carrying people into back surgeons left and right. We had fairly minor types of problems, but we had millions of them. They said there is an attitude associated with that which you have to deal with.

Another one of our corporate practices was for each plant to fill out a thirteen-category grievance report for corporate headquarters every month. The task force went through our grievance log. They inspected those thirteen categories. They pulled out all the grievances they felt had to do with safety that we had reported as discipline or something other than safety and came up with the conclusion that 71 percent of the grievances in Ionia had something to do with complaints about safety or the lack of safety.

They went through the MIOSHA inspection reports that we get back, and there were 25 or 30 of them during that two-year period. They found that there was not one single serious violation, nor one serious citation issued. There were a lot of situations mentioned—electrical boxes, tripping hazards, things like that—and there were a lot of reports that just had recommendations. They were not even citations. There were several that were merely reports that MIOSHA inspectors had been there, making no recommendations and no citations. And the task force concluded that there was an attitude problem and that that attitude problem was pushing our workers' compensation costs into seven figures annually and that it was something we had to deal with. And then, like all corporate task forces, they left. They went back to Akron with their report under their arms and said you guys have to handle this attitude problem.

SOLVING THE PROBLEM

So we looked at our problem with attitudes. We looked for things that we could readily control. We looked for things we could get the most immediate response from. And we looked for things that were right at the plant.

The first one that popped out at us was grievance activity. Would it be possible for us to control the grievance activity in the plant, to minimize it and get it down? We looked at how grievances were handled. The pattern was like this: The employee would come to the foreman and say, "I have a problem with XYZ." The foreman would say, "Fine. File a grievance." So the employee would file a grievance and put it in a box at personnel, thus making it a personnel problem, not a department problem.

So we organized a meeting of the top union committee and all the department superintendents. We got the contract out and we said we want to handle grievances close to the source, the way it is supposed to be done. We put together a training program for stewards and supervisors on how to deal with grievances, and we trained the stewards and we trained the supervisors. Then we went to the supervisors and said, "If you guys cannot handle these grievances in the first step, then we will let your boss take care of it in the second step because we are sure he is as capable of doing that as you are." Interestingly enough, all of a sudden, things that had previously wound up stuck in this grievance procedure for ten months before a hearing were being handled on the floor. So it seems that if you want to change things, just tell somebody that you will have their boss handle the problem if they cannot. It sure worked for us! Our grievance activity dropped dramatically, as Figure 2 indicates.

Figure 2.

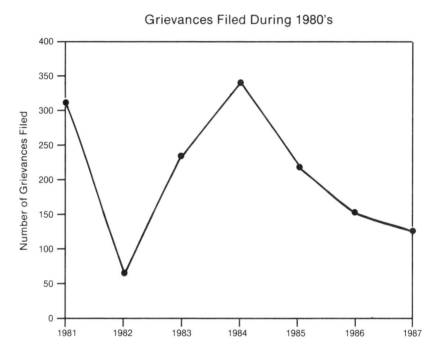

The second thing that we attended to was safety. We had had a company-union safety committee for as long as I had been with the company. It met when somebody asked when the last meeting had been. It was generally a one- to two-hour beefing contest, with complaints about this and that. We tried to improve the system, mirroring the MIOSHA pattern. We set up a system whereby people could go to that committee with a complaint or a concern about safety, either in person or in writing, individually or as a group or anonymously. We staffed that committee with the manager of maintenance and facilities, the chief maintenance planner and scheduler, so that when people came in with a complaint, it could be dealt with. That committee began to function in 1982 and for five years we did not have another MIOSHA inspection as a result of an employee complaint. The system has worked very well.

It is clear to us that by making our organization and our management at the plant level responsive to people's concerns about safety and health issues, we were able to effect a change in employee attitudes that was reflected in workers' compensation costs. Some of our attempts at change were certainly successful: grievances went down, lost-time accidents diminished, and workers' compensation costs decreased dramatically. Some things we never anticipated changing were also affected, like absenteeism. We had had an attendance-control program in place in the plant since 1977. We never changed it; we never re-emphasized it; we never did a thing with it. Yet when things started going better, when people started getting their problems resolved, absenteeism went down. It has been under 2 percent for the last three years, and under 1.5 percent for the last six months.

I think there is, as Ed observed a year or so ago, an interrelation between employee attitudes and things that indicate employee attitudes and workers' compensation. I think they go hand in hand and I think you can control and influence workers' compensation costs in your facilities without concentrating specifically on workers' compensation. In fact, if you concentrate on workers' compensation, I think you are at the wrong end of the problem. Your company's safety record and your people's opinion of how you respond to and deal with safety problems in the plant are what are going to cause attitudes to improve, opinions to change, and accidents and costs to go down.

PART THREE

Contributions from Government

PART THREE

7

View from the Top

Elizabeth P. Howe

The Michigan Department of Labor is especially proud to be taking part in this conference and publication. Its theme—cooperation and working together—is recognized nationally as the theme of Governor James J. Blanchard's administration. We are convinced that future progress in the areas of labor relations and economic development will depend upon joint cooperative efforts between workers and employers, union and management.

I am especially pleased to see this working in the area of workers' compensation. This was often thought of as a particularly difficult, troublesome, and antagonistic area, and it is encouraging to see so much interest in strategies that will lower employers' costs and reduce the suffering of workers at the same time.

We are proud that Michigan is a leader in this area. Michigan employers who have experience in successful techniques of this sort can be leaders in providing an example to others. All of us in Michigan can be leaders in showing everyone throughout the country how the workplace can be improved through cooperation. It is also encouraging to see people coming together from such diverse areas as state government, organized labor, the academic arena, and business enterprise.

I do want to take this opportunity to brag about a few specific things that have happened in Michigan.

Most of the time, the Michigan workers' compensation system works just right. Only about one-quarter of all cases involve a contest or dispute. About three-quarters of the time a worker is injured, reports the injury, receives medical attention, is paid benefits, recovers, and returns to work without any problem or dispute.

The number of contested or disputed cases has been cut in half in recent years. In 1981 there were more than 44,000 new contested cases each year. In 1987 there were only about 21,000. (It is important to point out that during this time there have been just as many injuries, which means that cases are being resolved voluntarily.)

Michigan is no longer a "high-cost state." Dramatic changes in Michigan's law during the 1980s have now put us in a place where we are competitive in the cost of workers' compensation insurance.

Michigan does what small business needs. A 1987 study conducted by the National Federation of Independent Business Foundation reported that Michigan has "one of the strongest explicitly competitive environments for workers' compensation insurance." The report noted substantial savings for Michigan employers, beginning with a 25 percent drop in 1983.

Competitive pricing is the best way to ensure that small businesses do not pay more than is necessary in premiums, the study concludes.

Group self-insurance is another option the study indicated states should allow. Michigan is one of the leading states in providing this alternative to a wide range of employers, according to the study.

Another effective method the report pointed to as important in keeping costs to business low is experience rating. Under this method an individual firm's workers' compensation insurance premiums are based on the firm's loss experience. Michigan is one of several states to offer this option.

The study confirms our belief that Michigan is a leader in standing by its small-business community to keep costs down. The report was conducted by James Chelius, faculty member at the Institute of Management and Labor Relations at Rutgers University, and Robert S. Smith, Professor in Labor Economics at the New York State School of Industrial and Labor Relations at Cornell University.

Employers can take advantage of competitive pricing. Workers' compensation insurance rates have been deregulated in Michigan since 1983. Since that time many employers are saving money by shopping around for the best price. More information about this is available in "Could You Be Paying Less for Workers' Comp Insurance?" by Pat Cannon, elsewhere in this book.

Mediation solves problems. Mediators are available in nine bureau offices to answer questions, provide information, and help parties solve disputes. More information concerning this program can be found in the chapter by John P. Miron, "Problem Solving Through Informal Conferences and Formal Mediation."

There's a bright future in store. Many employers are saving money through new approaches involving safety, disability management, and early return to work. The bureau is engaged in research and education programs in all these areas.

Probably one of the best things we can do to help keep costs in line while providing the best possible system for injured workers is to communicate with each other. From the success of this seminar, it looks like that type of cooperation is continuing.

8

Problem Solving Through Informal Conferences and Formal Mediation

John P. Miron

Mediation, like other forms of alternative dispute resolution, is often seen as a new fad; but the Bureau of Workers' Disability Compensation has been mediating cases informally for many years. It was an ongoing program when I got here, and I can attest to over 30 years. Back then mediation was accomplished through direct communication, ordinarily over the telephone. In 1970 we started a more formal type of case resolution on a limited basis. We hired two people to expand the ongoing system and called it a consultant program.

The consultants received phone calls and letters and interviewed walk-ins. We resolved problems similarly: by phone calls, letters, and face-to-face discussion. In 1981 the program was expanded to four people. Credibility became established with carriers, unions, and attorneys, and as the program expanded, it became more formal. Notices of conferences were mailed and the parties appeared at still informal conferences.

In 1985 major administrative changes were passed by the legislature. At this time the mediation program was formally included in the law, with a requirement that certain types of cases have a mediation conference before they could go forward in the litigation process. The types of cases for which the law mandates mediation are as follows:

- The claim concerns a definite period of time and the employee has returned to work.

- The claim is for medical benefits only.

- The claimant is not represented by an attorney.

- The bureau determines that the claim may be settled by mediation.

When the legislature added mediation to the statute, it also provided for the application form to be used to apply for mediation or for a hearing to include detailed information about the injury. At the time this form is filed, the worker must provide the employer any medical records relevant to the claim that are in his or her possession. Once the application is received by the bureau, it is served upon the employer and its insurance carrier. The employer must then file an employer's response form providing detailed information from its point of view and must send medical records in its possession to the worker or the worker's attorney. The response must be specific in its reason for denial of benefits. This exchange of information is very important to the success of mediation.

For mediation to be successful, the mediator must know the facts of the individual case. Medical reports must be understood, and for this it is sometimes necessary to talk directly to the doctor in more difficult cases.

It is important to remember that what is crucial is not what we as individuals think, but what the law provides. All parties must take time to know the workers' compensation law.

For mediation to work, the parties must come to the hearing with both knowledge and a spirit of resolution. If they do this, more than likely the mediation process will be a success.

Another key to the success of the mediation program is the informality in which it is held. There is no record made of the proceeding, and there is no decision rendered at the end of the process. Rather, it is an opportunity for all the parties to sit down with a mediator appointed by the bureau and examine all aspects of the case. It is a new way to get together to get the job done.

At the hearing the mediator encourages the parties to exchange all the information about the case. They then explore together the various possibilities for an agreeable solution to the problem. If the dispute is not resolved at the mediation hearing, the case is assigned a trial date before a workers' compensation magistrate.

I would like to emphasize that the bureau is still in the non-statutory mediation process, too. We encourage all parties to call upon us to assist in claim resolution even when a formal application has not been filed. As before, this includes phone calls, letters, walk-in visits, and conferences where the parties sit down together with a mediator. If a problem can be resolved before the formal litigation process is started, we believe everyone benefits.

We have all read articles in papers and journals discussing mediation. Barbara Ashley Phillips and Anthony C. Piazza prepared one such article, which appeared in the March 1985 issue of the *Certified Property Casualty Underwriters Journal*. Their article includes a list of the advantages of mediation which I think describes very well Michigan's workers' compensation mediation program:

- 'Claimants felt they had the equivalent of their 'day in court.'

- Claims representatives had the opportunity to evaluate the claimants and their testimony first hand, in an informal setting. This allowed a realistic evaluation of their credibility. . . .

- Both sides profited by the input of a neutral party on the relative merits of, or problem with, their case.

- The participation of the mediator helped resolve client problems for the attorneys. . . . Having the clients participate directly in the resolution process gave them a feeling of ownership in the resulting settlement.

- The dispute can be depersonalized. It is not uncommon for the settlement talks to stalemate because of personal antagonism between the representatives of the parties.

Even if a case cannot be settled at mediation, going through the process has advantages for both the employee and the employer. It is an opportunity to exchange facts, to re-establish credibility, and to learn from one another. In our view, mediation is the first giant step in bringing the system back from the legal entanglement in which we now find it.

DOES MEDIATION WORK?

Does mediation work? The statistics indicate that we held 4,600 statutory mediation hearings and almost 2,000 informal conferences in 1987, although the program did not get fully underway until March. We originally felt that if we could settle 25 percent of the cases, we would be doing well. In fact, as indicated in the table below, we did much better.

Table 1.

Method of Resolution	Percent Resolved	
	Statutory Mediation	Informal Conference
Voluntary Pay by Employer	24	38
Not Pursued by Employee	15	22
Total Resolved	39	60

In addition, the Mediation Division met with about 1,945 walk-ins and handled over 45,000 phone calls.

We want our mediators to be positive, objective, and appreciative. And we think you should be too. Mediation is here to stay in Michigan.

9

Could You Be Paying Less For Workers' Compensation Insurance?

Patrick D. Cannon

Over 5,000 Michigan employers will call the Bureau of Workers' Compensation this year to request information and guidance on reducing their workers' compensation costs. All who call will receive reliable information, and more than half of the employers will learn that, yes, they can reduce their workers' compensation costs.

Michigan employers are discovering that there is "Good News" about workers' compensation in Michigan today, that there have been changes that improve the system and make it function better for everyone. Slowly, but steadily, employers are learning that "comp" is not a nasty four-letter word—at least not anymore.

Before I joined the Michigan Department of Labor in January of 1987 I worked in the Michigan Senate for ten years. During that period of service as a legislative staffer, I became somewhat familiar with our workers' compensation system and the numerous reforms of the system over the years.

What I became most familiar with, however, was the realization that everyone was always criticizing workers' comp. Everyone! Or, at least it seemed that way. It seemed that the workers' compensation system was blamed for the faltering economy, high unemployment, rising inflation rates, the birth rate, divorce rate, death rate and the rise in juvenile delinquency. The state of our workers' comp system has also been blamed for plant closings, business leaving, new businesses locating elsewhere, workers coming into the state, and workers leaving the state. It seemed that just about anything that went wrong could be blamed, at least indirectly, on our state's workers' compensation system. To my knowledge, however, the system has not yet been blamed for prison overcrowding, Three Mile Island, or the Great Flood.

The blame came from all directions: from employers, employees, legislators, the insurance industry, the Chamber of Commerce, unions and, of course, most people you and I have ever known. Simply put, it became very popular—very easy—to point an accusing finger at workers' comp as the cause of most evils, most of the time.

As a legislative staff person, I had a chance to examine the system and learn that there were a lot of things "right" about workers' compensation in Michigan, particularly so since the 1982 reforms that brought competition into the selling of workers' compensation insurance. Indeed, our system, with all of its reforms, was a good one.

The opportunity for me to work for the Bureau of Workers' Disability Compensation surfaced in early 1987. The challenge was clear: help the business community, workers, and the public develop a better understanding of what our workers' compensation system is, and what it is not. It was a challenge I could not pass up; so I eagerly accepted the summons, knowing that changing attitudes about workers' comp would not come easily or quickly.

My initial task as Communications Specialist for the bureau was to develop a plan to reach people throughout the state with the "Good News" about workers' compensation. I was already convinced that businesses, workers and the general public could appreciate the good things about the system if they could only receive full and accurate information about it. I was also convinced that I could help business people reduce their cost for workers' comp insurance—if they had the right information.

One of the first outreach efforts of the bureau was the establishment of the Workers' Compensation Action Line, a toll-free telephone service that employers could call for information about workers' comp and guidance on reducing business costs. The next step was to promote the existence of the Action Line so employers would call and get the "Good News."

92 Today, I'm pleased to report, our Action Line is a busy service that is

helping businesses throughout the state in a variety of ways. In recent months we have been receiving between 400 and 500 calls per month and employers using the service are receiving good information about the system and are, as a consequence, developing a better understanding of what the system is and what it is not.

The calls we receive on the Action Line generally fall into one or more of five basic categories:

- Callers wanting general information about workers' compensation.

- People wanting to know who comes under the act and who must comply with its provisions.

- Employers wanting information about the cost of workers' compensation insurance.

- Employers and, in many cases, insurance agents wanting information regarding classification for coverage.

- Employers and employees wanting information or assistance with a specific workers' compensation claim.

In almost every case we are able to give the caller the information he or she is looking for or put the caller in touch with a person who can answer the inquiry. My office, for example, cannot access claim files directly; so inquiries regarding specific claims are generally referred to the bureau field office in the caller's specific area for assistance.

Most of the calls received on the Action Line are from Michigan employers, employers who are looking for help in securing workers' comp coverage and those who want help in reducing their costs for coverage. In many cases, those employers asking for help in lowering costs are quite skeptical—they're asking for help, but seem to doubt that someone in government is really going to offer it.

One of the greatest satisfactions in my job is helping that employer and putting that skepticism to rest. The fact is that employers calling the Action Line are getting helpful information—new information that helps develop a better understanding of what workers' compensation is and what it is not. Of course, the employers who are most satisfied with our service are those who save money as a result of their call—and I'm pleased to say that there are a lot of employers saving money because of the Action Line.

More than half of the employers calling the Action Line are paying more for their workers' compensation insurance than necessary! Armed with accurate information from their Action Line encounter, these employers can reduce their workers' comp insurance costs if they're willing to devote some time and energy to the mission.

In most cases, I have found that there are two major keys to reducing employers' costs for workers' compensation insurance: proper classifications and shopping around for the lowest rates. There are many employers in Michigan who still believe that the rates are set by the state and that it doesn't make any difference where their coverage is purchased. They simply don't know that they can save money—sometimes a lot of money—by checking around for the lowest rate.

One of the most significant changes in the workers' compensation system in recent years was the 1982 reform that permitted competition among insurance companies selling workers' compensation coverage. In the first three years of open competition, comp insurance premiums fell by nearly 40 percent. Today, despite rising insurance costs nationwide, most Michigan employers can pay less for their workers' compensation coverage than they did in 1980.

Most employers—perhaps two out of three, or even more—can reduce the cost of workers' compensation insurance by simply shopping for the lowest premium and obtaining classifications most appropriate for their business. There are more than 400 different employment classifications used in determining rates for workers' compensation insurance. In many classifications rates may vary by more than 50 percent.

More often than you might think, employers are not placed in the classification most appropriately suited for their particular type of business. The result, of course, is that these employers are paying more for their coverage than necessary.

I encourage employers to separate their payroll as much as possible to be sure that they're paying premiums in the class matching the work being performed. Furthermore, a single employee may be placed in more than one classification if it can be documented that the employee performs work suited to more than one class code.

A real-life example of improper classification costing employers money occurred this past year with a temporary employment service. This company hired clerical personnel and assigned them to various office sites in the area. These employees should have been placed in the 8810 classification at a cost of about 38 cents per one hundred dollars of payroll. Instead, this temporary employment service was placed in code 5610, which is designated as debris removal and construction site clean-up. The cost for code 5610 was $6.63 per one hundred dollars of payroll—about 17 times as much as they should have been paying.

Here's an example of how a bakery saved money by dividing its classifications. The classification for bakeries is 2003, with a premium cost of about $7.67 per one hundred dollars of payroll. However, several of this bakery's employees spent only half of their workday making bread; the other half was spent at the sales counter. By dividing the bakery's payroll, half of the premium cost could be charged to class code 8017 for retail stores, with a cost of about $2.09 per hundred dollars of payroll— less than one-third the cost of the bakeries classification. By dividing the payroll in this manner, a small bakery with an annual payroll of $100,000 would save about $3,000 in premium costs—and no matter how you slice it, that's a lot of bread.

Proper classification and prudent shopping are keys to insurance rate reduction. Once the proper class codes are determined, the next step is shopping around for the carrier with the lowest rates in those classifications. To assist employers in this effort, our office offers a comprehensive list of rates, compiled by the Michigan Department of Commerce, which shows the wide range of premiums charged for workers' compensation insurance, indexing manual rates by nearly 200 carriers for the most commonly used classifications.

The Workers' Compensation Action Line is not a household word around the state and we really don't expect it to be—at least not for a while. But we do hope that every employer in Michigan will some day soon know that the Action Line service is in place and ready to help with questions about workers' compensation and about how to reduce business costs.

As we continue to spread the word about the service, we're hopeful that thousands of employers will learn about the Action Line. Please help us: make a note of the Action Line number (1-800-523-7890) and tell other people about the service. Share our toll-free number with them and tell them the Action Line service is free. And please tell them that there is, indeed, "Good News" about workers' compensation in Michigan today!

10

Thirty-One Ideas For Improved Claims Handling

Ervin Vahratian

After having been directly involved in workers' compensation for many years, I am convinced that good management of a claim can breed success and that success reduces costs. For self-insured employers or insurance carriers writing workers' compensation, reducing costs can mean the difference between making and not making a profit.

There are several different avenues to successful management of a workers' compensation claim. Three, pictured in the equations that will follow, formulate the basis of our discussion.

```
Knowledge + Investigation = Success
```

The first essential element in the successful management of a claim is *knowledge,* although knowledge alone will never produce success.

Knowledge means being acquainted with truth, facts, or principles. Specifically, for claims handling this breaks down into the following rules of thumb.

- **Know the workers' compensation statute, including its interpretations.**

It is essential to be familiar both with the provisions found in the law and with the way courts and administrative agencies have interpreted those provisions.

- **Know the spirit of the law.**

One must know what the basic intent or idea behind the law was, whom it was designed to help, and how.

- **Know the practical application of the law.**

Many laws are never carried out in practice the way they are written in the statutes or the way they were intended by the legislature. This may be good or bad; but in working with the system it is important to know how the law is in fact applied in the real world.

- **Know and understand that the workers' compensation law is the exclusive remedy for employees and is intended to deliver benefits to disabled workers.**

The worker has given up his or her right to sue the employer in a civil court, and workers' compensation has been given in return as the exclusive remedy for injured workers. It is important to bear in mind that it is a system designed and intended to deliver benefits to disabled workers.

- **As the employer—know the employee and family.**

How old is the worker? What kind of training, education, or work experience does he or she have? What family factors are there that will influence his or her needs and disability? For example, is there a spouse at home who can take care of the injured worker? Are there young children at home who need day care? Are there older children depending upon a paycheck for their college education? All of these and many more factors will influence the claim.

- **As a carrier—know your policyholder and the employee and family.**

In addition to knowing the employee and his or her family, an insurance carrier (or third-party administrator) must know the employer. What kind of work is available in this plant? What kinds of attitudes are present in the top management? on the assembly line? Is there light work that can be given to an injured employee? Is the company willing to make accommodations?

Part of the process of gaining knowledge is an investigation. For successful claim handling, your investigation must be accurate, complete, and efficient. Through investigation you can get to know the employee, the employer, the issue of compensability, the medical problems related to the specific case, and the necessity of vocational rehabilitation, as well as the possibility of recovery from a third party.

Your investigation is a reflection of you: it indicates the way you think, the way you act, and your attention to detail. Remember that in most instances investigation is the primary step in the handling of any claim, and most claims cannot be processed without investigation. The purposes of investigation are twofold. First, you investigate for information and, second, you investigate for defense.

Reminder List—Investigation

- **No assumptions.**

Do not assume anything. Investigate. Find out what happened.

- **Get the employee's statement, in person or by telephone.**

The statement by the injured worker is crucial to any investigation. If at all possible, it should be taken in person; if not, then by telephone. Also, talk to co-workers. Find out what co-workers saw or did not see.

- **Notice.**

Michigan's Workers' Disability Compensation Act, like most similar laws, has a notice requirement. Often this is overlooked during an investigation. What notice was given? Where? When? By whom and to whom? Meeting the legal requirement of notice is often easy, but the way notice was given frequently can tell us a great deal about the claim.

- **Where did the employee go for first treatment? Was it to a company first-aid facility? To an emergency room? To a family doctor?**

This can tell a lot about the claim.

- **Are the injuries described in the medical report consistent with other medical records?**

Are the claims consistent? Did the first-aid nurse see evidence of what   **99** the employee claims he or she suffered? Did subsequent physicians treat for the same problem? Are the reports consistent?

- **Do not form preconceptions; only establish facts. Opinions are not facts.**

Everyone will have an opinion about what happened. Some may like or dislike the worker. They will trust or not trust the doctor or the nurse. These opinions may be of value, but it is important to separate them and treat them differently from the available facts.

- **If statements are taken, take negative statements as well.**

It may be important that there were people who did not see anything happen when other people claim a traumatic event occurred. It may be important that no note was made in the first-aid record.

Once you have developed your knowledge and investigation, you should correlate these into action. You are then at a point where you can resolve a human problem in workers' compensation and get the best possible result for the least cost. With knowledge and some understanding of what the problems are, you can begin to control the claims. It can be done. *Knowledge plus investigation equals success.*

Attitude + Communication + Commitment = Success

The employee's and employer's goals may appear to be diverse at first glance; but they are not. They both want to return the employee to productive employment as soon as possible, while the employee is intent on getting all that is coming to him or her and the employer is trying to fulfill the requirements of the law at the least possible cost. In my view, these goals are compatible. But to remain so, they require trust.

- **Trust is very important.**

A trusting relationship among the worker, the employer, and the carrier is the key to an early, successful resolution of any claim.

- **Share knowledge. Explain what happens under the workers' compensation law.**

Workers should be given a pamphlet published by their company about their rights and responsibilities under workers' compensation law before an injury ever occurs. Do not be afraid to tell the worker what his or her rights are. Be sure your workers know, for example, of their right to be reimbursed for mileage to a doctor and their right to choose their own doctor.

- **Advise of problems at the outset of claim.**

If there are problems involved in a case, talk to the worker about them. Don't hide this information.

In addition to trust, one of the most essential factors underlying good claims management is good communication.

- **Better personal communications will improve harmony and cooperation between the parties involved.**

Everyone will benefit accordingly.

- **Through personal communications you become better acquainted and you open the lines of contact.**

Open communication and an understanding of one another's positions and perspectives mean a great deal.

- **Individual personal contact makes people feel needed, respected, and liked.**

Such feelings help resolve problems. Whenever you have a personal discussion, it is important to show that you respect the other person. In addition, you must want to settle a disagreement or it will not be settled. In personal communication, another thing that helps is to have a funny bone up your sleeve.

Remember, diplomacy in communication is the art of letting someone else have *your* way.

Another important factor in successful claims handling is commitment— your commitment to your employees and to managing the claims. In terms of your employees, I have several suggestions.

- **Establish personal contact.**

It is important for you as the claims representative to establish personal contact with the employees. You must meet them personally; look them over and let them look you over. Gain their confidence. Show them you care.

As an employer, it is essential that you establish trust and communication with all your employees.

- **Maintain personal contact.**

If an employee is in the hospital or at home for an extended period, go and visit. This will establish good will that will go beyond settlement, regardless of the outcome of the claim.

- **Control through personal contact.**

First, you have to recognize and believe that if you can control the employee, your job will be easier. You will be more effective. Furthermore, this kind of control, which cannot be achieved or maintained without a conscientious effort on the claim representative's part, is indispensable to effective claims handling. The question that remains, however, is: How do you control an employee in workers' compensation?

- **Control through good care.**

Maintaining good medical care is the highest priority, because providing the best medical care establishes confidence. I believe that a claims representative or administrator should visit the doctors who are being used in workers' compensation, the hospitals that employees are referred to, the clinics that are used, and the local medical and vocational rehabilitation facilities. Initiate good contact and maintain good communications.

- **A combination of good care, good contact, and good communication will go far to establish good claims management.**

These things provide control over the case. When a case is out of control, the employee runs to an attorney, or in disgust to new doctors, and costs escalate.

Another element in good claims managment is the control of disability. The factors we have discussed so far—knowledge, investigation, attitude, communication, and commitment—all affect one's ability to control disability. Doing so is a challenge, but not an impossibility.

First, it helps to plan ahead and to practice good medical management techniques.

- **Know the level and quality of medical care provided.**

Become familiar with the on-site and off-site facilities available for medical care. Survey doctors' offices, clinics, and hospitals. Know what is provided.

- **Listen to complaints.**

If there are repeated complaints about the quality of care or the attitude of providers in your clinic, claims are probably not being handled properly there.

- **Is your medical team short-changing the worker?**

Are they rushing the employee back to work before the waiting period runs out, for example? If so, they may save you a few dollars in some claims but by building a poor attitude they will probably cost you a great deal more in the long run.

- **Do you review the type of care and facility from time to time?**

The person responsible for workers' compensation in every company should go to the health care facility on a regular basis and observe the level and quality of treatment.

- **Do you use medical cost containment?**

A great many new programs are available to deal with the rapid inflation in medical costs. Are you taking advantage of these?

- **Do not maintain a totally negative attitude toward an employee's treating with his or her own doctor.**

In Michigan, as in most states, the worker can choose his or her own physician after a certain period of time. Many companies assume that such a choice is bad and that it automatically indicates a breach of any good relationship that existed. This is not necessarily so. A physician is most likely to heal a patient who has confidence in him or her. Thus, it may be to everyone's advantage to have the worker choose a new physician.

Controlling claims by controlling communications, employees, and disability will assist you in getting good results. You must plan in advance. You cannot make haphazard decisions as cases come up each day. Good claim planning will reduce disability, and thus assist you in reducing costs.

Attitude has a great deal to do with success, not only in workers' compensation claims but in all lines of endeavor. Proper, courteous, and prompt servicing are all critical factors in achieving success. A philosophy that works, one that helps you get the job done and not procrastinate, is what this is all about. The only way to service a claim is the right way.

Success = Cost Control

Knowledge and control are powerful weapons when employed properly. With able people you have all the tools necessary in handling workers' compensation claims and in fulfilling the obligations of employers in this most human and difficult field.

PART FOUR

Thoughts from the Scholarly Community

PART FOUR

11

Differences in Workers' Compensation Costs

H. Allan Hunt

INTRODUCTION

As most of you already know, there is enormous variation among employers in their workers' compensation costs. This is unlike other social insurance programs, such as the federal Old Age and Survivors Insurance program (OASI) under which everyone pays the same tax rate although on different wage levels, or the state unemployment insurance programs, which—even with individual employer experience rating—have much more uniform charges than workers' compensation programs.

Many factors influence a particular employer's workers' compensation costs. Among the most significant of these are the employer's product line or industry, its recent accident experience, the location of its establishment, and its insurance arrangements.

- Industry has a tremendous impact, due to the accident exposures characteristic of different types of activities. There is generally a

50- to 100-fold difference between the safest and the most dangerous industry classifications within a given state. In Michigan in 1986, for example, while iron foundry employers experienced an average expected (pure premium) benefit-cost level of $11.85 per $100 of payroll, employers of clerical office workers expected to pay only $0.25 per $100 for the same basic coverage.[1]

- The individual employer's workers' compensation claims experience can also make a significant difference, particularly for those employers large enough to be subject to experience modification based on their own claims record. The range of actual annual premiums charged to iron foundry employers in Michigan in 1986, for example, was from $13.84 to $21.70 per $100 of payroll. For employers of clerical office employees, rates ranged from $0.20 to $0.48 per $100.[2] It would be normal to find at least a two-fold variation among employers within the same exposure classification in a given state.

- Location also makes a considerable difference in an employer's costs. There are dramatic differences among states, for example, as will be shown below. Workers' compensation costs are approximately three to five times greater in Minnesota than in Indiana for the same class of employer. There may also be sub-state differences, although information is not currently available to confirm this.

- The particular workers' compensation insurance arrangement is also believed to make a difference in the employer's cost of coverage. Careful selection of a carrier, or of the self-insurance option, may cause a potential difference of up to 25 percent for many insurance classes.

There is another area that has not yet received much public attention that may also have a very significant impact on these costs—the particular policies adopted by the employer to manage the human resources employed in his or her business. Employer policies toward the work force in general, and toward injured and disabled workers in particular, are now believed to play a substantial role in determining the claims experience and the subsequent cost of workers' compensation coverage for many employers. This promising new area, as it relates to disabled workers,

---

[1] Data on 1986 pure premiums supplied by the Compensation Advisory Organization of Michigan.

[2] Data are taken from the Insurance Commissioner's "Final Report and Certification of the State of Competition in the Workers' Compensation Insurance Market," Department of Licensing and Regulation, State of Michigan, August 4, 1987. It should be noted that manual premium is higher than pure premium because it includes all of the operating costs and expected profits of insurance companies, while pure premium only includes the expected benefit costs and loss adjustment expenses.

has come to be called "disability management." The term refers to a loose collection of policies and attitudes that may well distinguish employers who have very good workers' compensation experiences from those who have poor experiences.[3]

Disability management is characterized by attempts to identify and manage all significant disability risk factors, job modifications to prevent disability or to accommodate the disabled worker, early intervention in the disability process with aggressive rehabilitation efforts, and personnel policies that are designed to maintain the individual's connection with the firm after injury.[4]

The experience of some firms is reported as offering substantial reductions in the number of reported accidents and workers' compensation claims as a result of improved employer-employee relations. At the moment, no one can be sure of the general magnitude of impact of this relationship for a wide range of employers, but the obvious implication of the disability management movement is that employers can help themselves, rather than looking to the legislature or the insurance carriers for assistance in controlling workers' compensation costs. At the same time, the social payoff to such activities is clear since under disability management efforts the workers are less likely to be injured, more likely to return to work, and less liable to become disabled.

Because of the clear policy significance of this area, the Upjohn Institute— under the sponsorship of the Bureau of Workers' Disability Compensation of the Michigan Department of Labor—is currently studying the differences among employers in the incidence of workers' compensation claims and the contribution of private policy initiatives to these differences. We will describe this study briefly at the end of this chapter.

Trends in the Cost of Workers' Compensation, 1958 to 1984

The typical employer's costs of workers' compensation coverage in Michigan, in the seven other Great Lakes states, and in a 28-state "national" average on a consistent basis from 1958 to 1984 are estimated in Figure

---

[3] For a general introduction to the disability management field, see *The Journal of Applied Rehabilitation Counseling*, Volume 17, Number 3 (Fall 1986). This was a special issue devoted entirely to disability management and rehabilitation in the workplace, with guest editors Denise G. Tate and Rochelle V. Habeck.

[4] See the excellent bibliography developed by the Disability Management Project at Michigan State University, *Disability Management and Health Promotion: An Annotated Bibliography*, compiled and annotated by Denise G. Tate, Cynthia A. Hockett, and Jodi Starkman, edited by Lynn R. Allen (Lansing: Michigan State University, 1985).

1.[5] These estimates use a weighted average of the 44 workers' comp classes that are most general in occurrence; together they represent about 62 percent of payroll nationally.

Figure 1.

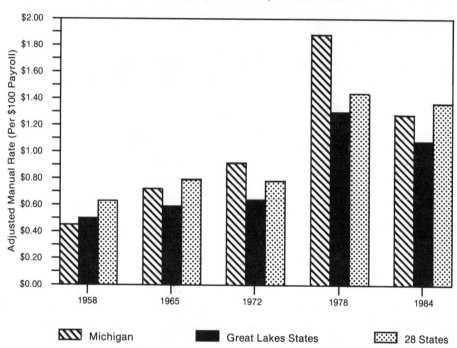

Workers' Compensation Insurance Costs
44 WC Classes, 1958 to 1984

The figure shows a long, steady rise in costs from 1958 to 1978, with the rise in Michigan being faster than in its neighbor states or in the nation as a whole. During this 20-year period, the cost of workers' comp insurance relative to payroll in Michigan quadrupled: the average rate rose from $0.45 to $1.89 per $100 of payroll. Of course, since payroll costs were rising at the same time, actual dollar costs of workers' comp coverage increased much faster than this.

Compared to neighboring states, costs in Michigan rose from 12 percent less than the average of the other Great Lakes states (Illinois, Indiana, Minnesota, New York, Ohio, Pennsylvania, and Wisconsin) in 1958 to nearly

---

5   See John F. Burton, H. Allan Hunt, and Alan B. Krueger, "Interstate Variations in the Employers' Costs of Workers' Compensation, with Particular Reference to Michigan and the Other Great Lakes States (Ithaca, New York: Workers' Compensation Income Systems, Inc., 1985) for a full description of the method and the data used in this analysis. It is the same basic methodology that Burton has been using for the last 20 years to compare workers' compensation costs across jurisdictions.

50 percent higher by 1978. Michigan rose from 27 percent below the national average to 33 percent above average over the same 20-year period.

It would be fair to say that the complaints of Michigan business leaders about these costs were heard in Lansing. In response, significant reforms of the Michigan workers' comp system were enacted in 1980 and 1981, followed by the deregulation of comp insurance rate-making in 1983.[6] Michigan rationalized benefit calculations, raised maximum benefits, eliminated minimums, repealed some irrational provisions (such as dependency and workweek presumptions), changed the definition of disability to send a message to the courts, added an aggressive coordination-of-benefits provision, and granted limited inflation protection for the long-term disabled.

As a result, there was a substantial reduction in costs, as can be seen in Figure 1: a net decline of nearly one-third between 1978 and 1984 pushed Michigan to slightly below the 28-state "national" average.
[Figure 2 about here.]

Figure 2.

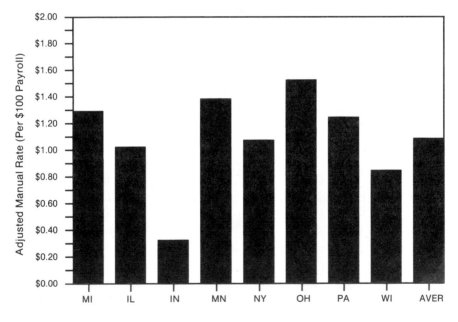

Estimated Cost of WC Insurance
44 Classes, Great Lakes States, 1984

---

6   See H. Allan Hunt, "Two Rounds of Workers' Compensation Reform in Michigan," in James Chelius, editor, *Current Issues in Workers' Compensation* (Kalamazoo, Michigan: W.E. Upjohn Institute for Employment Research, 1986) for an account of these reforms in Michigan.

Differences Among States in Workers' Compensation Costs in 1984

However, Michigan still had a regional problem with workers' compensation costs, a fact illustrated by the dramatic variation of costs across state lines, as shown in Figure 2. Examination of the individual states indicates that costs of insurance in Indiana and Wisconsin were substantially lower than in Michigan, for a standard set of classes and payroll weights. Illinois, New York, and Pennsylvania were also slightly lower. Among the Great Lakes states, only Ohio and Minnesota were higher than Michigan. Thus, in spite of the reforms, in 1984 Michigan was still 21 percent higher than the average of the other Great Lakes states.

As Figure 3 shows, this was even more true for manufacturing employers. Using the same basic method and time period to analyze 24 manufacturing classifications, our study shows that workers' compensation costs in Michigan were as much as 40 percent above those in the states that surround her.[7] Only Minnesota had higher costs for manufacturing firms in 1984. So it is clear that all workers' compensation costs do not move together. There is considerable variation both across states and over time in costs experienced across individual employers and time and space.

Figure 3.

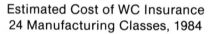

Estimated Cost of WC Insurance
24 Manufacturing Classes, 1984

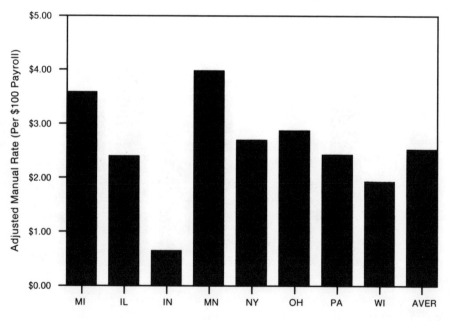

---

[7] Again, see Burton, Hunt, and Krueger, "Interstate Variations in the Employers' Costs," for full details of the methodology.

Intrastate Differences in Workers' Compensation Costs

Back in 1978, the Upjohn Institute collected a sample of Michigan workers' compensation cases for empirical analysis. We published a book called *Workers' Compensation System in Michigan,* describing what was found through a statistical analysis of some 2,200 closed compensation cases. I am pleased to say that many of the problems identified in that study were addressed in the subsequent reform efforts in 1981 and 1982.

One of the puzzles that emerged from that analysis, however, has never been resolved to my satisfaction. That is that litigation rates across Michigan varied radically by location. In particular, southeast Michigan (including Detroit) had much higher litigation rates than southwest Michigan.[8] (See Figure 4.)

Figure 4.

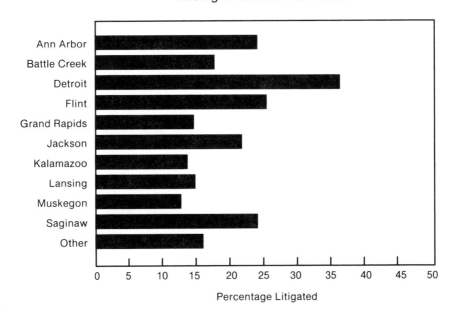

1978 Litigation Rates By Location
Michigan Closed WC Claims

Percentage Litigated

---

[8]   In Michigan, a workers' comp claim is designated "litigated" if either of the parties resort to the formal dispute resolution mechanism and request a formal hearing.

These findings led me to get involved in one of the minor skirmishes in the battle for the Saturn plant in 1986. Based on the data shown in Figure 4, I estimated that the difference in litigation rates alone could produce a workers' compensation cost differential of as much as 50 percent between southeast and southwest Michigan. Unfortunately, this wasn't enough to persuade General Motors to locate the Saturn plant in Michigan rather than in Tennessee, but it did raise some interesting questions.

It also led Ed Welch, Director of the Bureau of Workers' Disability Compensation, and me to start talking about what these differences really meant in a policy sense. If employers in southeast and southwest Michigan are operating under the same workers' compensation statute, but have such different experiences, what is driving the system? How can we explain such differences?

With help from Michigan State University, the Upjohn Institute is currently studying the differences in the incidence of workers' compensation claims in four industries in Michigan. We hope to isolate the range of variation among firms in claims experience and the environmental and policy causes of this variance. In short, we are looking at the role of "private policy" in reducing workers' comp costs in Michigan.

In this study we have tabulated the number of claims closed against individual employers in Michigan in 1986 and matched this number against the employment level of the firm that year. All employers were then ranked according to their closed claim incidence. Next we selected the best 15 percent and the worst 15 percent of those firms with over 50 employees in four industries (food production, fabricated metals, transportation equipment, and the health care industry) for further study. We will soon be gathering individual data from a sample of these firms for comparative analysis.

The sample will include both self-insured employers and those with commercial insurance. It will include large employers (with thousands of employees) and smaller units (with as few as 50 employees). It will include employers that are unionized and those that are not, and it will include employers from every part of the state.

Data are being gathered on the accident and workers' compensation claims experience of the firms, the characteristics of their labor forces, their attitudes toward the workers' compensation system, and their utilization of a number of specific disability management techniques. We are looking forward to learning more about these firms and what determines their compensation claims experiences. We are hopeful that we can make a significant contribution toward an understanding of what determines workers' compensation claims experience at the firm level.

This research promises to enhance our understanding of ways individual employers and their employees can control their workers' compensation costs . The public interest could be served by our identifying significant behavioral differences between the best employers and the worst employers in Michigan and then helping to develop a program to improve the practices of employers who are having bad experiences.

12

An Integrated Approach To Health in the Workplace

Daniel R. Ilgen

and

Scott N. Swisher

INTRODUCTION

At conferences like this one where the focus is upon addressing a particular problem, most of the attention is directed toward the description and evaluation of programs or particular courses of action people have developed to deal directly with the problem. This conference is no exception, nor should it be. The problem is a significant one. Who can quibble with the desirability of reducing worker suffering? If costs can be reduced in the process, all the better. Those of you who are facing that problem are eager to hear how others have treated it in order to learn something that you can take home and adopt into your own settings.

117

We too are interested in reducing worker suffering and costs. Unlike several others, however, we have no specific program to offer. Rather, we are suggesting a process for attacking the problem. This process is much more general than any particular program. This generality is a major advantage, but such advantages are purchased at a price. While the generality allows us to address a number of different issues related to worker suffering, it does not provide a particular program that can be applied immediately to address a specific problem. We make no apologies for our perspective; we simply want to make our approach explicit at the outset.

Our purpose is to present a systems perspective for addressing health at work. To do this we will first briefly describe past approaches to health as a contrast to the systems perspective. We will then present a systems model of medicine—known as the biopsychosocial (BPS) model—as the primary guide to our perspective. Next, we shall describe the implications of the use of such a model. And, finally, we shall describe a joint project between Michigan State University and the Swedish Employers' Confederation (SAF). This project involves a group of ten medical doctors who are working closely with us to be trained in the biopsychosocial model; these doctors, who are specialists in industrial medicine, plan to conduct research back in Sweden on issues of worker health from a biopsychosocial perspective.

APPROACHES TO HEALTH AT WORK

Past approaches to health at work can be seen as a progression that began with a concentration on safety and evolved to the current focus on wellness (see Figure 1). At the turn of the twentieth century, as muckrakers were quick to point out, work in industrial plants was dangerous, often even life threatening. By the late 1930s and early 1940s, public concern led to the creation of governmental agencies such as the National Safety Council and other units like the Industrial Fatigue Research Board that were set up to address safety and to develop safe working conditions.[1] Workmen's compensation plans were also devised then to provide aid for workers who were injured on the job. These early efforts took a mechanistic, causal approach to safety by looking for conditions that were likely to influence the safety of employees and then attempting to change them. The nature of cause was viewed as unidirectional—from the job environment to the worker.

---

[1]   M. S. Viteles, *Industrial Psychology* (New York: Horton, 1932)

Figure 1.

Approaches To Health At Work

Model   Target of Concern

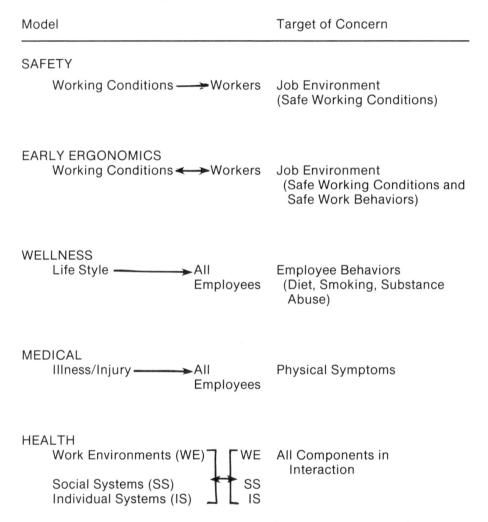

SAFETY
      Working Conditions ──►Workers   Job Environment
                                       (Safe Working Conditions)

EARLY ERGONOMICS
      Working Conditions ◄──►Workers   Job Environment
                                       (Safe Working Conditions and
                                       Safe Work Behaviors)

WELLNESS
      Life Style ────────►All   Employee Behaviors
                          Employees   (Diet, Smoking, Substance
                                       Abuse)

MEDICAL
      Illness/Injury────────►All   Physical Symptoms
                             Employees

HEALTH
      Work Environments (WE)┐ ┌WE   All Components in
                                       Interaction
      Social Systems (SS)   ↕ ↕ SS
      Individual Systems (IS)┘ └IS

Changes and regulations that resulted from the early safety research and legislation were extremely beneficial. Although such industries as agriculture, mining, meat packing, and construction still remain relatively dangerous in comparison to other types of work, there is no question that safety-related accidents have been reduced by the changes made in those industries' working conditions. In many respects, however, the visible signs of change were due as much to the severity of the original working conditions as to the correctness of the model that drove the **119** approach to improving health through reducing hazardous working conditions.

The focus on safety gave way to what we have labeled as early ergonomics. The major changes from the safety model to that of early ergonomics were the inclusion of the workers in the response to safety and health and the recognition of the interaction between work environments and those who populate them with respect to maintaining safe working conditions. Thus, attempts to improve the safety of the workplace included training of the workers in safe behaviors, the development of incentives to encourage safe behaviors, and the selection and placement of persons on jobs with safety and health in mind. The early ergonomics view is perhaps best captured in the regulations and practices spawned by the Occupational Health and Safety Act (OSHA) of 1970 and the regulatory agency it created. The agency plays a major role in regulating the nature of the American workplace today.

In the late 1970s and early 1980s, the early ergonomics model gave way to the current ergonomics model, most frequently labeled "wellness." This model represented two major changes from the previous approaches. First, the primary concern of the wellness model shifted from that of preventing injury or harm to that of encouraging health. Prior to the wellness approach, health was defined primarily in terms of the absence of injury or disease; with the new model, the absence of disease or injury was seen as the neutral point on a scale running from illness or injury to health. The illustration in Figure 2 illustrates a wellness continuum as construed under that perspective.

The second change in emphasis with wellness was that of looking to the individuals, rather than to conditions at work, as the primary precursors of health. How employees behave (what they eat or drink and how much exercise they get, for example) is the focus of wellness programs, not conditions in the work environment. The programs are directed either at changing unhealthy behaviors and replacing them with healthful ones or at establishing healthy behaviors in the first place. Typical health-related behaviors targeted by wellness programs are diet, exercise, smoking, and substance abuse. More important to our point here, however, is the general orientation. In contrast to previous approaches that looked to working conditions for the causes of unhealthy outcomes with attempts to change the conditions or change the people to deal with the conditions, the wellness approach focuses almost exclusively on changing behaviors believed to increase the likelihood of illness or other forms of incapacitation at some time in the future.

Figure 2.

The Continuum from Illness to Wellness.

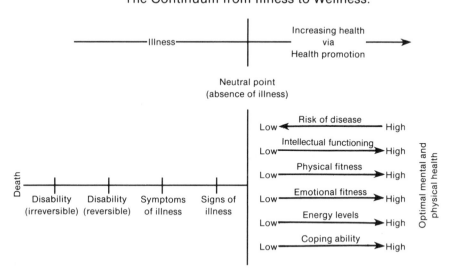

Source: G.S. Everly and R.H.L. Feldman, eds. *Occupational Health Promotion* (New York: Wiley, 1984).

The fourth model illustrated in Figure 1 is the medical one. This well-established model does not fit into the chronological pattern established by the first three models; it predated all of them, spanned the whole time period, and is very much with us today. Typically, workers with symptoms or findings of illness are referred to medical doctors who treat them by following the standard practice of first attempting to diagnose the source of the symptoms and then providing medical treatment to address the problem. The relationship between the worker and the doctor is the standard patient-doctor relationship similar to that present in most other medical situations.

EVALUATION OF PRACTICES

Without a doubt, past and present practices related to health in the workplace have made great strides. Changes have been made to make the workplace safer and less likely to produce physical harm. Training and placement have improved workers' ability to deal with potentially dangerous conditions. Likewise, improving the healthful behaviors of people should lead to improvements in health; but whether most people can be trained and motivated to change well-established unhealthy behaviors in the long run is not so clear. Finally, the accomplishments of medical science are well documented. These distinct and usually unrelated approaches have contributed and continue to contribute a great deal to the health of people at work.

There are, however, several limiting features shared by all these models, the most severe being the reliance on rather simplistic cause-and-effect models of illness and health. These models assume that there exists a set of variables that either alone or in simple interaction with one another cause the condition that is of concern. This type of model is most clearly apparent in medicine, where illnesses are assumed to result from a single cause or a limited set of causes. Under this assumption, when the causes are unknown, medical research looks for them. Once the cause is isolated, attempts are made to combat it. Small pox, measles, and polio are just a few of the many cases to which medical science can point to show that the biological model of medicine has been applied successfully.

This model works best when the causal determinants of the disease are few in number. The major causes of death today, however—cardio-vascular diseases and cancer—are believed to result from a complex combination of biological, psychological, and social factors. As a result, more complex interactive models are now needed.

Problems with complex causality, which demand more complex models, can just as easily relate to safety. Consider the case of handling potentially hazardous chemicals, for example, where long-term effects of the chemicals on workers are a function of biological differences among people, the social acceptance of the means of protection from the chemicals, and the personal stress experienced by the individuals, as well as by other variables that interact in ways that do not fit simple linear cause-and-effect models. Thus, there is a need for an expanded view of health at work that is better able to incorporate the complexities of the problems being faced.

A second limitation of most of the work in all of the four models described is that they espouse a concern for health but rarely address it. For the most part, the absence of accident, injury, illness, or other physical, psychological, or behavioral symptoms of sickness is taken as a surrogate measure of health. However, as was pointed out by Everly and Feldman, among others, health goes beyond the absence of illness, with the latter being a necessary but not sufficient condition for the former.[2]

SYSTEMS VIEWS

The biopsychosocial model with which we are working has its origins in general systems theory. The general system that involves man is a hierarchical system arranged in ascending order of complexity, as illustrated in Figure 3. Complexity is defined as the number of possible interactions of the elements that exist at a given level. Similar systems can be developed with other entities at their center, as man is at the center of this one.

In general, a given level in such a system interacts primarily with one or two levels above and below it. These interactions are usually the most important and the easiest to delineate. Less common interactions may occur with more remote levels, and phenomena occurring at the more remote levels may initiate a propagating chain of changes that affects other levels indirectly.

The implication of this type of model is that in general one must understand the levels above and below one's primary level of interest in order to understand its phenomena. This is particularly true in the operational sense: a change induced at one level will have implications for other levels. This view is fundamental to such disciplines as ecology where Barry Commoner has coined an aphorism, "everything is connected to everything." It is the adjoining connections, however, that are usually the most significant.

As previously noted (see Figure 3), the practice of medicine has classically been based on the biomedical model. The focus was on man and downward levels of organization. Science in this respect was primarily reductionistic in perspective and in its research tactics. There were many successes, but problems accompanied many of these apparent victories. There developed an increasing fragmentation of knowledge, without apparent ways of integrating it. Many biologically based "victories" presented new problems. For example, control of measles among small children in some areas of the Third World has further fueled their population explosions and increased the threat of starvation, which is primarily a sociopolitical and economic problem. Thus, these dimensions of the problems of an infectious disease are inextricably related, and disease prevention at primarily a biological level fails, if one's criterion of success is improved

---

[2]   G. S. Everly and R.H.L. Feldman, eds., *Occupational Health Promotion* (New York: Wiley, 1984) and J. Cullen and C. G. Sandberg, "Wellness and Stress Management Programmes: A Critical Evaluation," *Ergonomics,* Vol. 30 (1987): 287-94.

Figure 3.

Hierarchy of Man and Science

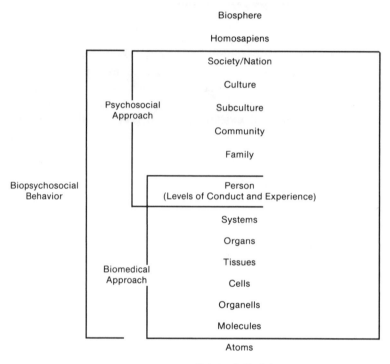

Biosphere

Homosapiens

Society/Nation

Culture

Psychosocial Approach — Subculture

Community

Family

Biopsychosocial Behavior

Person (Levels of Conduct and Experience)

Systems

Organs

Tissues

Biomedical Approach

Cells

Organells

Molecules

Atoms

Subatomic Particles

Quarks

welfare of the individual and the population as a whole over the long term.

The complexity of health care has increased greatly in the era following World War II. Science has expanded our range of knowledge explosively, and technological applications of this information have followed in its footsteps. To apply this new base of science and technology, specialism of health care workers, primarily physicians, has increased at a rapid rate. Today even so-called subspecialties are further subdividing.

There have been sweeping economic and organizational changes in health care delivery systems, too. Many of these are motivated by economic considerations the new technology has brought into focus. These changes are of great significance both to employees and to their employers. Industrial medicine, the formal practice of medicine in the workplace, has been influenced by many of these changes, but not in a fundamental way as yet.

The expectations of people about their health care and their own role in decisionmaking have also had a profound influence on delivery systems and health workers. People are better educated, more aware of both the choices to be made and the factors they perceive to have an influence on their health status. One of the clearest of these new demands by people is attention to them as individuals, to their concerns, fears and needs, and to the requirement for open communication. The development of alternative types of health care that specifically reject most of the biomedical perspective is testimony to the depth of these feelings in our culture today.

DEVELOPMENT OF THE BIOPSYCHOSOCIAL MODEL

The biopsychosocial model developed in the period following World War II. It grew out of an area of research directed at classical disorders, most of which had no well-defined single factor cause. Researchers thought that psychological factors were important in the etiology of these disorders, and thus grew the so-called "psychosomatic medicine" of that era. Other thinkers, notably George Engel and his colleagues, saw a much larger perspective in which social factors also became of importance when one considered many problems in a broader and deeper way. By the mid-1960s the biopsychosocial perspective was well formulated and adopted in a number of medical schools as a central curricular theme. The College of Human Medicine of Michigan State University was one of the new medical schools that developed its curriculum and practice around this model. Acceptance of the model has slowly spread to medical education, practice, and research. For the most part, some aspects of the model are found in most medical schools and in some practice settings.

The basic tenet of the biopsychosocial model is that all phenomena related to health and disease have three inextricably related dimensions: the biological, the psychological, and the social. A triaxial reference system, such as that pictured in Figure 4, may be useful in conceptualizing this model. Every "event" can be plotted somewhere in the space defined by these axes. The relationships between these events can be represented as vectors. The scales assigned to the axes can be defined by the problem under consideration, but at some conceptual level, a universal relativistic scale of sorts must exist. This representation should not be taken beyond the limits of its usefulness, however, as a simple model of matters of great complexity.

Figure 4.

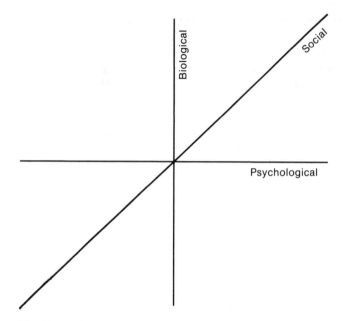

The biopsychosocial model as a three dimensional space in which events and phenomena can be plotted as vectors.

Finally, we should reconsider the concept of a "patient," classically regarded as an individual. Under some circumstances a related group of people could be regarded as a collective patient, as, for example, a family or a community in which a communicable disease has broken out. This concept of the collective patient is applicable to the workplace where individuals or work groups or even the company as a whole may be regarded as patients as they all seek to recover from illness or injury or to improve their individual or collective health.

The health care team must be redefined to include a much wider range of individuals and groups who have relevant information or skills that can be brought to bear on significant problems. They must work as a team, not as a collection of individuals each doing a specialist "thing." This will require significant cross-training among the members so that the big picture emerges rather than the small bit of a seemingly isolated problem. There must be high levels of communication to ensure the coherence of the group's approach and common, jointly determined goals. Above all, there must be leadership, and in the best of organizations this is shared in the same sense that goals and methods are chosen. The leadership also has responsibility for evaluation of the functioning and

126

results of the team and for using this information to improve procedures and to adapt to new requirements, which an ever-changing environment imposes.

The health model listed at the bottom of Figure 1 is meant to illustrate the systems perspective of the biopsychosocial model. In particular, it suggests that health is a complex interaction of the biological system represented in the individual, the psychological domain also primarily within the person, and the job and non-job environments incorporating physical and social systems. The social system includes other individuals both on and away from the job. The important point from a systems perspective is that health cannot be understood from the point of view of any one of the systems in isolation.

Figure 5.

Cycle of Environmental Effects
and Employee Health

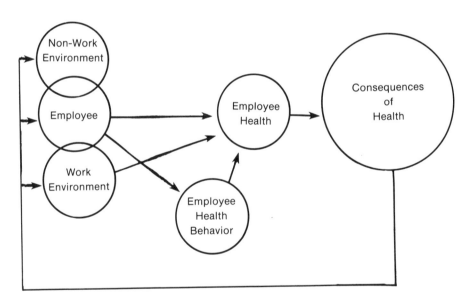

An alternative way to view the health model is illustrated in Figure 5. In this case, it is suggested that the employee resides in two circles of influence, a work and a non-work environment. The environments are composed of technological, biological, and social factors that impact upon him or her. From a health perspective, the primary concerns of this influence process are their effects on the employee's behaviors that affect health and upon health directly. An example of the former would be smoking and of the latter would be a virus in the environment that leads the individual to catch a cold. It is further suggested that the employee's health would then have consequences that feed back and affect the work or non-work environment or the individual himself or herself. An understanding of health is not possible without embedding it in the total set of systems in which it is located.

IMPLICATIONS OF THE SYSTEMS PERSPECTIVE

A systems perspective contributes to attacking problems of health at work in at least four ways (See Figure 6). The first of these is that it provides a frame-of-reference for thinking of health issues. By delineating the systems that are believed to be important for the health-related problem of interest, a systems perspective identifies a number of variables that are likely to impact on or be correlated with the problem. In addition, the nature of the interlocking systems suggests a structure or order for looking at the problem. Consider, for example, the systems illustrated in Figure 3 that are in descending order of size and ascending order of specificity. One of the features of such an order is that variables likely to have the greatest impact (to control the most variance) in the problem of interest will be located in the same system as the variable of interest, or in adjacent systems. That is, with few exceptions, covariation among variables is more likely to be greater for variables from systems closer in the hierarchy. Thus, a formal ordering of variables applying a logical process of facet analysis and the general rule of proximity leads to a set of hypotheses about the order of magnitude of effects as one attempts to discover information about a particular problem. Thus, the systems view provides guidance for addressing the problem.

Figure 6.

Implications of a Systems View of Health at Work

• Creates a Frame-of-Reference/Point of View

• Identifies or Addresses New Problems

• Broadens the Set of Actors

• Demands a Broader Base of Skills and Knowledge

The systems frame-of-reference also protects one from expecting simple solutions. Most health-related problems are complex and yet the desire for a quick solution to a pressing problem is great. The result of this combination is that we are often vulnerable to jumping to a premature conclusion. A systems perspective provides some protection against this by inducing a healthy skepticism against "quick fixes."

The second advantage of a systems perspective is related to the first: the perspective broadens the search for variables when confronted with new problems. If single-minded approaches to problems are used, then new problems lead to a search for solutions in the same domain. However, from a systems perspective, problem solutions are sought in multiple domains simultaneously. A good example of a new health problem in the work force that demands a systems attack is that of AIDS. A purely biological view would search for treatments primarily through medical science. However, it is clear that AIDS must be approached from a biological, psychological, and social perspective if there is to be any hope of slowing its spread. In fact, in the near future, greater effects are likely to come from social and psychological influences than biological ones.

Third, systems perspectives broaden the set of actors involved with addressing and maintaining health at work. The twentieth century has been a time of specialization. As the problems faced by human resource management in general and health maintenance in particular were recognized for their complexity, the trend has been to train persons to greater and greater levels of specialization. A systems perspective by no means denies the need for complex and fine-tuned technical skills to handle many of the problems of health at work. Dieticians, physical therapists, physicians, experts in contract negotiation, psychologists, psychiatric social workers, and others have all contributed to the quality of and concern for health at work. At the same time, a systems perspective leads to some caution regarding the efficacy of "solutions" to health problems from within any one of these disciplines. It also suggests that the pool of persons that have legitimate skills to offer to health care problems is more than likely broader than those typically related to addressing health.

Finally, a systems view demands a broader base of skills and knowledge from those involved in health at work. By this, we do not mean to imply that there is a need to return to the day of the generalist. Nor do we suggest that people are capable of being specialists across a broad band of topics. However, we do suggest that a narrow band of specialization is not sufficient to deal with complex systemwide problems. This means that, at the individual level, specialists must be aware of some of the major concepts from other systems outside their own area of specialization in order to perform effectively even *within* their own discipline. To accomplish this, all those concerned about health at work need to have a working knowledge of issues outside their own area of specialization. For example, as will be described further below, our own interests have been with managers and physicians. We will argue that physicians working with health at work and typically trained with specializations almost entirely within biological systems must have a knowledge of organizational systems in order to function effectively. They must understand issues of budget control systems, production, and technological and social systems in which their patients work in order to understand some of the types of health-related problems likely to be encountered. In our opinion, physicians cannot afford to limit their knowledge only to medicine. In a similar fashion, a manager well trained in the topics typically addressed in schools of business administration cannot deal effectively with human resources without some knowledge of hypertension, alcohol abuse, AIDS, stress, and other health factors in today's organizations.

THE MSU-SAF PROGRAM

Over the past eighteen months we have been involved in an effort that attempts to apply the systems model to the training and development of medical doctors. This effort began out of the common interests of Dr. Scott Swisher of the Department of Human Medicine at Michigan State University (MSU) and Dr. Carl Sandberg of the Svenka Arbetsgivaren-foreniningen (SAF) in Stockholm. Dr. Swisher's work on the biopsychosocial model of medicine came to the attention of Dr. Sandberg, who was trained as a psychiatrist, holds a position requiring that he work closely with management and labor on problems of industrial health. Dr. Sandberg was attracted to Dr. Swisher's work in large part out of his frustrations with the limitations of the classical biologically driven medical model for dealing with the problems he encountered in industry.

As a result of their correspondence, a joint project between MSU and the SAF was begun. The SAF is a large governmental agency in Sweden charged with addressing a number of issues related to human resources in the Swedish work force. The project began with a group of ten Swedish physicians who were working in industrial medicine as practiced in Sweden, not as practiced in the United States. Physicians in industrial medicine in Sweden are aligned neither with labor nor with management. Their charge is to work to maintain and improve the health of the work force more from a social welfare point of view. Therefore, some of the management-labor conflict that can interfere with the physician's task in American industries when he or she is an employee of management is avoided in the Swedish setting. Given that, we felt that the setting was a good place to begin work on training physicians in a systems perspective and evaluating the advantages of such an orientation. In particular, we felt that the unique contact these physicians had with members of the work force put them in an excellent position to identify and recognize problems or potential problems related to the health and welfare of that work force. Our theory was that if they had a greater knowledge of the other systems with which they interacted, particularly the management, technological, and social systems of the work setting, they would be better prepared to impact on these systems in ways that would benefit the health and welfare of all. In an ideal sense, we would like to see physicians play an additional role of change agent in the organizational setting rather than simply one of responding to workers who come to them with reports of physical ailments.

The MSU-SAF program is an ongoing one that began with two primary purposes. The first of these was that of instructing the physicians in the broader systems model. The second was to initiate some joint research projects between members of the MSU faculty and participants in the program who were to apply the principles being taught. In the spring of 1987 the group from Sweden came to MSU for two weeks of instruction in the systems approach and for initial development of the research projects. They returned again for one week in the fall of 1987. The next phase will be a two-week combination of research and instruction to be conducted in the early fall of 1988.

Several aspects of the systems perspective training conducted in Sweden are worth noting. (See Figure 7 for a list of selected topics from the MSU-SAF conference.) First, as would be expected, the participants were

Figure 7.

Selected Topics from the MSU-SAF Conference

- Historical and Theoretical Bases for the BPS Model
- The Key Role of Communications: The Interview
- The BPS Model in Clinical Medicine: AIDS as a Paradigm
- Health as a Concept and as a "Diagnosis"
- Approaches to Management and Behavior in the Workplace
- Socialization and Sense Making
- Careers and Career Development
- Work Motivation
- An Expanded View of the Industial Physician
- Formal Decision Analysis
- Ethical Issues in Industrial Medicine and Research
- Communications among Subcultures: Health and Management
- The Introduction and Management of Change

immersed in the nature and meaning of the biopsychosocial model. Next, the participants were given training in interviewing, despite the fact that all the participants had had years of experience with patient interviews from a medical perspective. This was because our research had shown that two characteristics of this experience tended to interfere with applying the BPS model. First, most probing by physicians is directed toward a search for biological causes for physiological symptoms. However, given the premise of the BPS model that the psychological and social setting are very likely sources for physiological symptoms, there was a need to sensitize the physicians to cues about possible sources of problems in other domains.

Second, the typical doctor-patient interview is one-sided, with the doctor as the expert maintaining a great deal of control over the process and often asking directed questions demanding "yes" or "no" responses. With the broader BPS model assumptions, we feel that the patient must be given more freedom to consider and describe a wide range of issues in his and her life that are unlikely to be easily anticipated by the physician but that, once mentioned, may be seen as potential sources of the physical problems reported by the patient. As a result, the interview process advocated is less directive than the typical doctor-patient interview; instruction and practice was provided in this process.

The final aspect of the training illustrated in Figure 7 is that of the business- or management-related topics. The social system in which those in industrial medicine are immersed is that of the world of work. Far too often, physicians in the work world know little about that social system. It is not uncommon for such physicians to have an office on site in a plant that looks and functions much like a physician's office at any other site. Clients come and go in manners that barely reflect the fact that this office or these clients are in an industrial setting. As a result, it is possible for the physicians to know little about important features of the work setting. Yet, understanding the social system of work is necessary for those who hope to incorporate that understanding into the treatment of illness and health at work. Thus, to provide greater exposure to the world of work, topics such as approaches to management, socialization, career development, and the management of change were introduced into our training. Our hope is ultimately to enable physicians to intervene and initiate changes that might improve health in such settings.

As was mentioned earlier, a second feature of the MSU-SAF project was research. The physicians were asked to generate research ideas that would be developed jointly between members of the MSU faculty and the Swedish participants and then conducted by the Swedish physicians at their home worksites. These projects were expected to incorporate features of the BPS model by addressing the issues from the standpoint of more than one system. As an example, one project involves attempts to encourage behavior change regarding smoking and alcohol consumption. This problem is being addressed from a biological-psychological systems angle, a social perspective, and a workplace view. In the biological systems perspective, a physical exam including laboratory tests for each participant precedes the educational program directed at reduction in smoking and drinking. A psychological component of the program is the feedback of physiological data to participants over time. Our social perspective includes an assessment at the workplace and among family and friends of the degree of social support that creates pressure both to smoke and drink and not to do the same. Finally, we are looking at physical conditions at the workplace that might encourage or discourage such behavior.

An interesting example of such encouragement exists in the Swedish approach to the treatment of smoking on the job. The smoking habit has long been considered in Sweden to be a condition that leads to an involuntary need for satisfaction. Therefore, although workers are not allowed to smoke on the job, special areas are provided for smoking, and, more importantly from our standpoint, workers are allowed to leave the job to smoke whenever they desire. Non-smokers are not given such freedom to leave their work space. Thus, smoking gives a worker some control over the work environment that is not present for non-smokers. This creates a disincentive for smoking cessation that must be addressed if the health-related behavior is to be successfully affected.

In this example the particular features of the research are less important than the systems perspective it represents. Thus, once knowledge is gained about factors affecting the health-relevant behavior of smoking, the next step is to intervene in ways that will improve health. In this instance, one possible change would be to intervene in the structuring of such practices as the control over breaks to give non-smokers similar controls. In general it is hoped that as physicians possess broader systems perspectives and skills for dealing with several systems, they can enter more actively into the change process.

CONCLUSIONS

Our purpose here was two-fold. First we wanted to espouse the need for a systems perspective for approaching health at work. This need arises from the fact that health issues at work are multiply determined. Therefore, attempts to address these issues from within a single system are, at best, limited and, at worst, misleading.

Our second purpose was to describe the MSU-SAF program as a prototype of a systems approach to health targeted at physicians. The goal of this **133** program is to equip physicians better for dealing with health at work and for becoming proactively involved in structuring work environments, both physical and social, to foster healthy working conditions.

Although our work to date has been limited to physicians, we see them as only one of a number of key actors in the drive to improve health at work. The specific features of a systemic perspective for other actors obviously would differ from those for physicians. However, we would argue that the basic model is the same. That is to say, the greatest advances will be made by individuals who are expert in their own area but who have more than a passing knowledge of how multiple systems impact on health. Such broad understanding would make these individuals better able to address health problems within their own domain by modifying and augmenting their approach to incorporate and fit the demands of other systems. It is this broader systems process that we feel will produce greater improvements than have been possible from our past parochialism.

13

Ethical Issues Relating To Workers' Compensation

Daniel H. Kruger

A democratic society exists for the welfare of the individual. The exciting history of the United States begins, in fact, with a declaration to promote the general welfare. Workers' compensation is an outstanding example of legislation designed to do just that. Initially enacted in Michigan in 1912, the Michigan Workmen's Compensation Act was the first state statute that dealt with two major problems of workers who had been injured on the job—the loss of income and the need to have medical benefits compensated.

The framers of this historic act were visionaries. They foresaw the development of what I call "the job economy." Since then the United States has become a nation of employees. Approximately 90 percent of the nation's labor force currently are employees. A nation of employees places great value on having a decent job, because a good-paying job produces an impressive array of economic, sociological, and psychological benefits for the individual job holder. A nation of employees needs a comprehensive workers' compensation act that is administered effectively and efficiently.

Workers' compensation, which is a mandated legal benefit for the bulk of employees, has both economic and psychological benefits. A worker who has been accidentally injured (or killed) on the job faces the reduction, interruption, or possible termination of his or her income-earning capacity. In addition to the income loss, the worker may well have incurred sizable medical expenses. An unexpected disabling illness or accident thus places a drain on the worker's financial resources. The economic dimension of workers' compensation is the payment of weekly benefits for income replacement because of injury or illness arising out of the course of employment and the payment of all medical expenses incurred.

There are important psychological benefits to workers' compensation, as well. It allays fears occasioned by an interruption of the income stream by giving the worker a feeling of "economic security." It creates certainty out of uncertainty. The fears and uncertainties that adversely affect the psychological well-being of the injured worker are minimized by workers' compensation.

Michigan was fortunate to have advocators, legislators and a governor who saw the need for a workers' compensation act in 1912. Seventy-five years later, it would probably be impossible to enact such progressive social insurance legislation. How sad! It is doubtful that employers, unions, and the other parties involved in workers' compensation could reach a consensus on such a comprehensive piece of legislation in 1988. Can you visualize the parties agreeing to the concept of injuries and illnesses arising in and out of the course of employment? or the definition of disability? or the level and duration of benefits? or unlimited medical expenses? Although it is true that the Michigan workers' compensation act was extensively revised in 1969, I call these revisions merely "fine tuning" of the 1912 act.

THE ACT AND THE SYSTEM

It is important to stress that there are both a workers' compensation act and a workers' compensation system. They are separate and distinct. The act passed by the Michigan legislation and amended over the years stands by itself and is an outstanding example of social engineering. The system, on the other hand, is a heterogeneous composite of many interest groups: employers, unions, physicians, employer associations, state labor federations, insurance carriers, lawyers, the state administrative agency for workers' compensation, the mediators employed by the state administrative agency, the administrative law judges, the appellate body provided in the act, legislators, the governor, and state court judges at all levels. It is the interaction of these many interest groups that constitutes the system.

Many of these interest groups come into play only after an injured worker files a claim. A claim filed by a worker or his or her estate can end up in the Michigan Supreme Court. A decision of the supreme court can trigger efforts to amend or change the law. Efforts to change the law evoke and involve a babel of voices and interest groups, each with their own axe to grind. These include unions, state labor federations, employers of all sorts, state Chambers of Commerce, state manufacturing associations, carriers, the state agency, legislators, the governor, and law firms, which lobby for their clients' vested interests.

The system has so many vested interests and so many different voices that the original intent and purpose of workers' compensation are lost, at times. Lest I sound too harsh, let me assure you that this distinction between the workers' compensation system and the workers' compensation act is not unique. The same observations can be made about the unemployment insurance system, the welfare system, and the Social Security system. The emergence of complex and powerful systems, with all kinds of vested interests, have almost paralyzed the Great American Society. There is no consensus on anything. The many actors are often incapable of reconciling vested interests to satisfy a public interest or the general welfare.

One way to view the workers' compensation system in Michigan is as a multi-interest bargaining relationship, in which the various groups bargain with each other in an effort to further their own interests. The voice of the injured worker is frequently muted by these conflicting vested interests.

The act, on the other hand, is neutral. It is not perfect; but it does represent a consensus reached by the legislature with the approval of the governor at some point in time. The act imposes both responsibilities and obligations on the injured worker, the employer, and the carrier, if the employer is not self-insured.

Since the workers' compensation act is the only statute society has available to deal with the problems of workers with occupational illnesses and injuries, it is of crucial importance that every effort be made to assure that the system works effectively and efficiently so that the intent of the act will be carried out. To accomplish the objective, the workers' compensation system must have integrity.

INTEGRITY

Workers' compensation is a process through which a series of inputs is converted into a certain output. The inputs include such procedures as a worker filing a claim, thorough investigation of the claim, and a physician providing medical services, if needed. These inputs are examined and massaged by employers, carriers, and administration agencies, and should result in appropriate benefits as prescribed by law. It should be a quality process, which has complete and total integrity. When the process lacks integrity, both workers and their employers have no confidence in it and thus have difficulty accepting the outcome it provides.

At times the process is contaminated by the state courts giving an extremely broad interpretation of what constitutes a compensable illness or injury under the act. A case in point is the significant growth in psychological disorders, which the courts have declared to be compensable as occupational illness. Currently, stress is a growth industry in the United States, and there is an army of "experts" ready for a fee to advise Americans and their employees how to handle it.

According to the National Council on Compensation Insurance, stress on the job now accounts for about 14 percent of occupational disease claims.[1] Thus stress or psychological disorders on the job are having a significant impact on workers' compensation. In my view, this interpretation has opened Pandora's Box. It is difficult to isolate stress on the job from stress generated by non-work situations. One disturbing aspect of the growth of stress cases is that it will inevitably lead to an erosion of the worker's privacy. Employers, in defending themselves, will begin to pry extensively into the private lives of their employees for root causes of stress. Employee off-duty activities will be scrutinized for stress-producing possibilities.

The workers' compensation act is an entitlement program based on right, yet there is another dimension to workers' compensation. Once an injured worker files a claim under the act, this creates what I call a "psychological contract." The claimant has a contract with the workers' compensation system and he or she expects that contract to be honored, just as he or she expects the claim to be paid. The psychological contract is unwritten; it is implied. It is a set of expectations and perceptions the claimant has. The contract is operative at all stages of the process, from the filing of a claim to its payment. It deals with how the claimant is perceived and how he or she is treated; it deals with all of the interveners and facilitators in the system, such as claim-takers, investigators, physicians, and carriers, who touch the claimant in some way during the process. The psychological

---
[1]   *The Wall Street Journal* (April 7, 1988): 31.

contract focuses on trust or mistrust, credibility or non-credibility, dignity or rudeness, a personal relationship or an impersonal one. The psychological contract is the human side of workers' compensation. The law, administrative rules, and court decisions are silent on the psychological contract and its administration. Yet, it is how the psychological contract is administered that gives workers' compensation its reputation and its image—good or bad.

In turn, the workers' compensation system places certain obligations on the claimant. The claimant must be truthful; the claimant must have "clean hands" if he or she wants the psychological contract to be honored. Employees need to be made aware of the penalties of filing a fraudulent claim. The act is not for workers who have injured their backs on snowmobiles or while skiing. Workers' compensation is not a program to supplement retirement benefits; it is not a mechanism to cheat the employer or the "System."

There is a critical need to educate the employees on the ABCs of workers' compensation. This benefit is a legislative mandate and not the result of collective bargaining. The program is fully paid by employers; the employees do not contribute one penny to its costs. The unions do not bargain for increased benefits or for laxities in administration. The benefits provided are uniform, whether in a unionized or non-union plant.

A VARIETY OF CONCERNS

One of the problems in introducing ethical behavior into the workers' compensation system is that there are multiple interests and multiple perceptions. The worker is concerned with workers' compensation's paying medical expenses and cash benefits. The employer is concerned with its costs. Insurance carriers are concerned with making or maximizing profits, pursuant to old-fashioned economic theory. Lawyers are concerned with workers' compensation as a money machine to be used to produce revenue for their firms and themselves (another variant of the old-fashioned economic theory of maximization). Some physicians see workers' compensation as an area in which no one is looking over their shoulder, either in terms of fees charged or of the quality of medical services provided. Employer associations, the legislature, and the governor are concerned with workers' compensation as a critical determinant of the "business climate in the state."

The business climate issue merits an additional comment. There is fierce interstate competition for new plants, and the cost of workers' compensation has been a salient point in enticing industry to locate in **139** a given state. This has resulted in the workers' compensation system becoming adversarial. Unions want higher benefits and a broader interpretation of compensable injuries and illnesses. Employers and the state economic development authorities want costs held steady or reduced.

Although these strong differing concerns have created an adversarial relationship within the workers' compensation system, I maintain that there is much room for collaborative interaction. There is also a need for greater emphasis on the ethical behavior of the actors in the system.

Since it appears that the workers' compensation system is analogous to collective bargaining, perhaps it would be useful for the parties to develop a list of practices to guide them in their interactions. These would certainly include the following:

- The actors in the system must bargain in good faith.
- The actors and other parties must present full disclosure.
- There will be no intimidation or coercion of a claimant.
- The claimant must be treated fairly and equitably.

Perhaps, in addition, there should be an amendment to the workers' compensation act to provide penalties for unfair claim processing. Arizona has recently amended its statute to provide for these situations.

In sum, the claimant has a set of obligations that must be met: to be truthful, and to file only a bona fide claim arising out of the employment relationship. The system likewise has its obligation: to honor the claimants' psychological contracts. Both the integrity and the image of the workers' compensation system would benefit from such behavior. But bringing integrity, credibility, believability, and ethical norms to the workers' compensation system cannot be legislated; it must be effected by individuals' behavior.

The workers' compensation act is an integral element of what I call the Responsible Society. The central goal of such a society is to strengthen and enhance human values. There is no magic formula to building the Responsible Society. What is required is for all elements of American society to respond fully to the needs of individuals in their roles as workers and citizens. In the process of responding, the society becomes responsible. The same formula can be applied to building a Responsible Workers' Compensation System, and herein lies a unique opportunity for all those involved if they so will it.

Index

D

E

F

Federal Express, 42, 44
Fitness programs, 33, 34, 45-46
Fraudulent claims, 4, 44, 48, 139
Funding, 59 (diag.), 60

G

Galvin, Donald E., 7
General Motors, Saturn plant, 114
General Tire and Rubber, 76
Government contributions, 7
Government perspective, 81-104
Grievance activity, 75 (fig.), 75-76, 78-80

H

Handicapped employees, 13, 15-16
Hazardous working conditions, 120
Health environmental effects, 127 (fig.)
Healthletics Program ⓈⓂ , 6, 23-37, 46
   advantages, 31-32
   cost per employee, 34-35
   cost savings, 27, 29-31
   employee participation, 28
   equipment, 26, 32-33
   injury index ratio, 30-31
   injury trends, 29 (fig.)
Health at work, 117-134
   approaches, 118-121
   evaluation of practices, 121-123
   systems perspective implications, 128-130
   systems views, 123-125
Health Data Institute, 45
Health insurance, 39-40
Health programs, 57-64
Heart disease, 122
Howe, Elizabeth P., 7
Hunt, H. Allan, 1
Hypertension, 130

I

Iacocca, Lee, 41, 45
144   Ilgen, Daniel R., 7

Illinois, 110, 112
Incentives, 20, 49, 120
Indiana, 1-2, 108, 110, 112
Industrial Fatigue Research Board, 118
Industrial medicine, 19 (fig.), 26 (fig.), 130
Injury intervention programs, 30. *See also* Healthletics Program (SM);
    Prevention
Institute for Rehabilitation and Disability Management, 44
Insurance
    as a cost factor, 107-108
    claims, 19 (fig.)
    competitive pricing, 85, 92, 94
    deregulation, 85, 111
    health, 39-40, 41
    industry classification codes, 94-95, 108
    insurers, 7
    Old Age Survivors Insurance, 107
    premiums, 7, 35, 84, 94-95
    rehabilitation services, 50
    self-insurance, 47, 84, 108
    workers' comp, 84, 91-95
Interstate differences, 1, 109-112
Intrastate differences, 1, 113-115
Investigation of claims.*See* Claims handling

K

Kruger, Daniel H., 7

L

Light duty.*See* Medical restrictions
Litigation, 7, 14, 88, 113 (fig.)
Location as a cost factor, 107, 108
Long-term disability, 17
Loyalty, 69, 71

M

Maine, 1-2
Malpractice liability, 35
Management support, 18, 48, 58-61, 63, 66-68.*See also* Corporate culture
Meade, Kevin, 6
Mediation, 85, 87-90
Medical model, 13-14
Medical restrictions, 3

Sawisch, Leonard P., 7
Seniority, 5
Sheltered workshops, 5-6
Siegel, Bernie S., on cancer patients, 3-4
Small businesses, 84
Smith, Robert S., 84
Smoking, 119 (fig.), 120, 127, 133
    in Sweden, 133
Soule, Jim, 3
Staffing, 59 (diag.), 60
Steelcase, case study, 3, 65-71
Stress, 50, 130, 138
Substance abuse, 40, 51, 69, 119 (fig.), 120, 130
Supervisors
    returning employees, 5
    support services, 48
    training, 48
Support services for supervisors, 48
Svenka Arbetsgivarenforeniningen, 130
Swedish Employers' Confederation, MSU- SAF Program, 118
Swisher, Scott N., 7, 130
Systems model, 15-18

T

3M, 50
Thurow, Lester C., on health care cost containment, 41
Tonti, Don, 6
Tracking systems, 20-21
Training
    doctors, 130-132
    employees, 62, 122
    stewards, 78
    supervisors, 48, 78
Transitional workshops, 5-6, 49, 68-69
Trust, 100
Turnover, 45, 69, 71

U

Unions, 140
    grievances, 75-76, 78
    joint committees, 79
    joint programs, 61
    reasonable accommodations, 12
    return-to-work program participation, 48
    seniority rules, 5